EAT THIS BOOK

D1569185

Critical Perspectives on Animals: Theory, Culture, Science, and Law

Critical Perspectives on Animals: Theory, Culture, Science, and Law
Series Editors: Gary L. Francione and Gary Steiner

The emerging interdisciplinary field of animal studies seeks to shed light on the nature of animal experience and the moral status of animals in ways that overcome the limitations of traditional approaches. Recent work on animals has been characterized by an increasing recognition of the importance of crossing disciplinary boundaries and exploring the affinities as well as the differences among the approaches of fields such as philosophy, law, sociology, political theory, ethology, and literary studies to questions pertaining to animals. This recognition has brought with it an openness to rethinking the very terms of critical inquiry and the traditional assumptions about human being and its relationship to the animal world. The books published in this series seek to contribute to contemporary reflections on the basic terms and methods of critical inquiry by focusing on fundamental questions arising out of the relationships and confrontations between humans and nonhuman animals, and ultimately to enrich our appreciation of the nature and ethical significance of nonhuman animals by providing a forum for the interdisciplinary exploration of questions and problems that have traditionally been confined within narrowly circumscribed disciplinary boundaries.

The Animal Rights Debate: Abolition or Regulation? Gary L. Francione and Robert Garner

Animal Rights Without Liberation: Applied Ethics and Human Obligations, Alasdair Cochrane

Experiencing Animal Minds: An Anthology of Animal–Human Encounters, edited by Julie A. Smith and Robert W. Mitchell

Animalia Americana: Animal Representations and Biopolitical Subjectivity, Colleen Glenney Boggs

Animal Oppression and Human Violence: Domesecration, Capitalism, and Global Conflict, David A. Nibert

Animals and the Limits of Postmodernism, Gary Steiner

Being Animal: Beasts and Boundaries in Nature Ethics, Anna L. Peterson

Flight Ways: Life and Loss at the Edge of Extinction, Thom van Dooren

EAT THIS BOOK

A Carnivore's Manifesto

DOMINIQUE LESTEL

Translated by Gary Steiner

Columbia University Press
New York

Columbia University Press
Publishers Since 1893
New York   Chichester, West Sussex
cup.columbia.edu
Apologie du carnivore © 2011 Les Editions Fayard
English translation © 2016 Columbia University Press
All rights reserved

Library of Congress Cataloging-in-Publication Data
Lestel, Dominique.
[Apologie du carnivore. English]
Eat this book : a carnivore's manifesto / Dominique Lestel ; Translated by Gary Steiner.
pages cm. — (Critical perspectives on animals : theory, culture, science, and law)
Includes bibliographical references.
ISBN 978-0-231-17296-7 (cloth : alk. paper) — ISBN 978-0-231-17297-4
(pbk. : alk. paper) — ISBN 978-0-231-54115-2 (e-book)
1. Meat—Moral and ethical aspects.   2. Vegetarianism—Moral and ethical aspects.
3. Human-animal relationships.   4. Animal welfare.   I. Title.

TX371.L4713 2016
641.3′6—dc23
2015028156

Columbia University Press books are printed on permanent and durable acid-free paper.
This book is printed on paper with recycled content.
Printed in the United States of America

c 10 9 8 7 6 5 4 3 2 1
p 10 9 8 7 6 5 4 3 2 1

COVER DESIGN: Milenda Nan Ok Lee
COVER ART: © iStockphoto

References to websites (URLs) were accurate at the time of writing. Neither the author
nor Columbia University Press is responsible for URLs that may have expired or
changed since the manuscript was prepared.

Just as philosophy begins with doubt,
a human life worth living begins with irony.

—Søren Kierkegaard

Contents

Translator's Preface

HOW CAN ONE POSSIBLY RECONCILE the seeming contradiction between the proposition that we human beings are bound together with animals in a condition of mortality and vulnerability and the proposition that we human beings have an affirmative obligation to eat meat? How can one sincerely claim to love and respect animals but also maintain that eating meat is not only permissible but downright obligatory? This question lies at the core of Dominique Lestel's reflection on the question of the animal, a question that has never had more urgency than it has today. In this connection, I am reminded of Heidegger's trenchant observation that "questioning is the piety of thinking"—that what is at stake in the task of critical reflection is not so much the ascertaining of definitive answers as an appreciation of, a dwelling within, and a willingness to endure the discomfort of questions that leave us feeling threatened and uncertain.[1] For I am made extremely uncomfortable by Lestel's suggestion that meat eating in some form is a human obligation, and yet I also feel a responsibility to confront the many questions that his suggestion raises, all of which devolve upon one singular question—the question of the animal.

In contemporary as well as in historical thought, this question has taken many different forms and raised many additional questions: What is animality? Is there one underlying essence that constitutes or defines animality or rather an irreducible multiplicity of manifestations of it? Are there any definitive, or even provisional, differences between human beings and nonhuman animals? On what grounds have so many people, in so many different cultures, considered human beings to be fundamentally superior to animals? (On what grounds, for that matter, do so many people think of human beings as *not* being animals?) On what grounds have so many people, for such a long time, treated animals as little more than resources to be used at our whim? Why do so many of us exhibit utter indifference to the exploitation and suffering of billions of animals every year? Why do we treat our pets so well but view so many other animals as expendable resources? Are there cultures that assert a fundamental parity or kinship between human beings and animals rather than seek to assert a fundamental human superiority? And if there are, why have these cultures not been more influential in humanity's historical reflections on questions of humanity, animality, and the relationship between the two? Can any sense be made of the proposition that we share an existential kinship with animals but that we nonetheless owe it to ourselves *and to them* to kill and eat animals, at least under certain circumstances?

Lestel's answer to the last question is yes. The central argument of *Eat This Book: A Carnivore's Manifesto* is that, as counterintuitive as it may sound, the only way to do genuine justice to animals, the only way to repay the infinite debt we owe animals, is to engage in what Lestel calls "ethical carnivorism." Human beings and animals share a common fate: to be mortal, to be vulnerable, and to be able to exist only on the basis of the death and consumption of other living beings. Now one might suppose that the best way to do justice to animals would be to *refrain* from killing and consuming them; after all, we have long considered a peaceful, nonviolent existence to be preferable to a destructive one. From the parable of the Garden of Eden to the Golden Age story proffered by the likes of Hesiod and Ovid, our culture has long claimed that the essence of humanity consists in its ability to rise above the violence and destructiveness of wild nature and establish civilization on the principle of nonviolence and mutual respect. From this it would appear to be a short step to the conclusion that if we truly care for animals and see them as our kin, the best thing we could do to demonstrate our concern and respect for them would be simply to leave them alone—at the very least to eschew altogether the consumption of meat and perhaps all other animal products as well. Ethical vegetarians and vegans take the view that it is cosmically unfair to include only human beings and to exclude animals from an ethic of nonviolence. Not only logical consistency but genuine respect for animals demands that we practice nonviolence toward them just as we at least purport to practice nonviolence toward our fellow human beings.

Lestel calls this line of reasoning radically into question. Where ethical vegetarians and vegans believe that they are embracing and acting on a principle of purity and piety, Lestel offers another interpretation altogether, one that challenges the ethical vegetarian's claim to piety and urges on us an entirely different picture of what it means to act in a reverential manner toward the animals on whose lives our own lives depend.[2] In Lestel's view, it is not the meat eater but rather (and precisely) the ethical vegetarian who subscribes to the doctrine of human exceptionalism, the view that human beings are fundamentally superior to animals and the rest of nature. To see ourselves (and ourselves alone) as capable of rising above nature and attaining a kind of transcendent purity is to forget the underlying, tragic terms of existence: that life is forever predicated on death and that human beings are every bit as entangled in a web of mutual interdependence as every other living being. The ethical vegetarian seeks to wish away this fact and in doing so would make it impossible for us to acknowledge and repay the infinite debt that we owe to animals for our very existence. Thus, the ethical vegetarian, if only entirely unwittingly, reinforces the sense of human exceptionalism rather than militating against it. What is needed most is not a denial of the terms of existence but rather their open embrace, and this is what ethical carnivorism affirms.

Lestel has argued vehemently and at length in his writings for something very much like what I have argued for in my own writings—namely, a fundamental cosmic kinship with animals that confers on us deep ethical responsibility toward them.[3] But the two of us come to diametrically opposed conclusions about the ethical implications of cosmic kinship. Lestel pushes for a "spiritual ecology" that in some ways recalls Aldo Leopold's land ethic.[4] The terms of this spiritual ecology entail an ethics of reciprocity between human beings and animals whose terms can be fulfilled only through active and conscious participation in the cycles of generation and destruction that define life. This means, Lestel argues, that human beings *must* eat meat if they are to fulfill their moral obligations.

In advancing his ethics of reciprocity between human beings and the rest of the living world, Lestel derives inspiration from holistic cosmologies such as that of the Algonquin of North America. He sees in these traditions a recognition and embrace of the fact that human life and death are inextricably bound up with the life and death of other earthly creatures. Peoples such as the Algonquin kill and eat animals, but they do so in a spirit of reverence and sincere thankfulness to the animals who sacrifice their lives so that humans may live a little longer. The same spirit of reverence characterizes Lestel's ethic of reciprocity; thus, contemporary practices such as animal experimentation and factory farming, far from being ethically permissible, stand as testimonials to the utterly irreverent posture of contemporary human beings. Lestel's call for ethical carnivorism is a far cry from current attitudes toward meat eating. The United Nations Food and Agriculture Organization reports that more than fifty billion land animals worldwide are killed and consumed by human beings every year, and many of these animals are raised in horrifying conditions. Lestel is well aware of this fact, and he argues unremittingly for the cessation of invasive animal experimentation and factory farming. We must eat meat in order to acknowledge the infinite debt we owe to animals, but we must do so in a spirit of modesty and humility, and we must endeavor to minimize or avoid animal suffering as far as possible.

All this might sound like some sort of straightforward answer or formula for discharging our ethical responsibilities toward animals and the living in general, but in fact it ultimately leaves us with an unanswered question. That Lestel himself is aware of this is hinted at in his choice of epigram for the book, Kierkegaard's remark about the importance of irony in a life well led—not to mention the importance of doubt in philosophical reflection.[5] Does Lestel actually believe that meat eating is an ethical imperative? He offers his reflection on the ethics of meat eating as a provocation to those of us writing about animal rights to step back and raise anew the question of the animal and its many subquestions. As he notes in his postface to the book, what is most needed sometimes in exigent circumstances is the exploration of possibilities that seem the most counterintuitive. And the circumstances of animals today are nothing if not exigent.

A final word about this book concerns my reasons for having undertaken the task of translating it. Given the lengths to which I have gone in my own work to argue for veganism as a strict ethical obligation, the reader must be wondering what would have motivated me to translate a book whose central thesis is so at odds with my own thinking. The reason is simple: Lestel is one of the most trenchant and thought-provoking thinkers writing about animals today, and English-speaking readers who are genuinely concerned about the moral status of animals need to take his ideas into consideration. The measure of the importance of a text or an idea is not whether in some objective sense it is "correct" or whether it corroborates the conclusion at which I am invested in arriving, but rather whether reflection on it helps us to move closer to the truth. So much of what passes for intellectual discourse today exhibits not an openness to opposing ideas but rather a determination to silence ideas that go against the grain. The best way to test one's own convictions is to open oneself completely to the challenge posed by one's most strenuous critics or opponents—to confront doubt rather than to seek to extinguish it and to attempt to dwell in the space of irony. If what we are interested in is the truth rather than winning arguments, we must lend a sympathetic ear to voices that challenge and unsettle us. For me, Dominique Lestel's is one such voice. And it is very much worth listening to.[6]

A Sort of Apéritif

THERE WAS A TIME WHEN UNBRIDLED sexuality raised the ire of right-thinking people who had a strong desire to lead others onto "the right road." The strange passion for hygiene on the part of those who wish to exult in a surfeit of morality has always sought expression in the metaphors of the *Michelin Guide*. Different times, different morals. Today, those who have become vegetarians for ethical reasons harass carnivores in the same way that militant members of temperance leagues once pursued women of easy virtue.

Indeed, contemporary morality is adding a new prohibition to its long list: for some people, eating meat is not far from committing a crime. Opponents of this practice maintain that it is possible and even necessary to proscribe the regime of meat entirely, just as one is forbidden to kill his neighbor. Thus, the choice to be vegetarian is viewed not as a personal choice but rather as a categorical imperative, in the Kantian sense of the term, that is to be followed unconditionally. Whoever makes a different choice necessarily descends into evil. Consequently and entirely logically, the ethical vegetarian wants to obligate others to rally to his position: by means of persuasion in the first instance, by making those who continue to eat meat feel guilty, and subsequently by means of the law and coercion, if need be.

For the ethical vegetarian is a moral fundamentalist ready for anything. Am I exaggerating? Here is an example of what the dubious reader can get between her teeth if she takes the trouble to consult the literature ad hoc. Estiva Reus and Antoine Comiti wrote in the *Cahiers antispécistes* (Antispeciesist journal) in February 2008: "The thesis defended in this article is that we must henceforth work explicitly toward the legal prohibition of the production and consumption of animal flesh. This is both a necessary measure and one that can be achieved without waiting for a revolution in people's sensibilities or in the organization of our societies."[1] The forecasted utopia has the colors of vegetables and the consistency of fruits. Abstaining from eating animals is supposed to lead to ultimate redemption: bring an end to suffering, become kind, save the planet, and finally nourish all the destitute inhabitants of creation. The intentions are good, but, as they say, that's what the road to hell is paved with.

My previous book, *L'animal est l'avenir de l'homme* (The animal is the future of the human), provided intellectual tools to defenders of animals, but these tools were often ridiculed. Although the present essay has a similar spirit, its radical critique of ethical vegetarianism may cause surprise. Indeed, we have a tendency to believe that loving animals and not wanting to eat them are two inseparable attitudes. But such an inner compatibility is far from obvious. However legitimate and virulent the vegetarian posture may be, it remains surprisingly poorly conceptualized and leads to some paradoxes that few if any vegetarians are prepared to accept.

Thus, in the following pages I defend a thesis that is somewhat complicated and may be shocking at first glance. The ethical vegetarian's position is tenable only if it is radical, but its very radicality is completely unacceptable for the majority of vegetarians. For this position is antianimal. Here at the beginning of the twenty-first century, it revives the great frontier traced between human and animal by putting it into up-to-date terms, even though everything today shows any such frontier to be insubstantial. Nonetheless, the majority of vegetarians I know sincerely love animals. Such a contradiction poses a problem.

In this essay, my reflections are directed exclusively at *ethical* vegetarians. Thus, I refer to those who believe that it is evil to eat meat particularly on the grounds that such consumption is based on murder, suffering, and egoism. The ethical vegetarian's position appears excessive to many people, and it certainly is excessive. It remains to know why. Those who are vegetarians as a matter of taste or for sanitary reasons interest me no more than someone who thinks he or she will become more intelligent by eating chocolate or more beautiful by bathing in the ocean: to each his or her convictions!

Even if I do not share their beliefs, ethical vegetarians appear to me to be more worthy of interest; in a word, I sense in them a certain perversity that excites my predatory instinct.[2] Thus, it is to them and to them alone that I make reference here when I speak of the vegetarian.

One can criticize the vegetarian position with very strong arguments that vegetarians must take into account in order to remain credible. At the same time, vegetarians greatly underestimate what it means to be a carnivore. In fact, they never so much as pose the question. In particular, I suggest that the vegetarian's love of animals—a love that the carnivore supposedly lacks—could redound to his disadvantage. The vegetarian is accustomed to believing that his struggle is sufficiently just that he need not think about it but only spread the word. He sees himself entirely in terms of a force relationship with the carnivore, when in fact there is also a genuine intellectual controversy. And this controversy, contrary to what the majority of militant vegetarians believe, is not without value. Properly explored, it can only strengthen considerably what they have to say and help them to understand better what they want to say.

Many people consider the vegetarian to be good, the carnivore to be a brute, and the defender of the carnivore to be a villain. This is not simply a basic summary of the prevailing attitude; more than anything else it is false.[3] The arguments of those who would like to consume only vegetables, fruits, and cereals for ethical reasons are often highly questionable. At the same time, the carnivore is sometimes closer to animals than a vegetarian can ever be because she completely accepts (i.e., accepts metabolically) her animal nature rather than becoming disgusted with it. Notwithstanding my infinite respect for animals and the importance that I accord them, I challenge the idea that killing a nonhuman animal can be classified as murder. Terminological confusion is always a first step toward barbarism, and the recognition of this fact was one of the British writer George Orwell's most brilliant insights. It is of more than passing interest that he would have applied this idea in precise terms to relations among animals. Thus, it is important to reverse the ethical vegetarian's demand by showing that in fact it is eating meat that is an ethical duty. We call this the *carnivorous imperative.*

Eating meat can be considered an ethical duty for the Westerner inasmuch as it is an action that reinscribes the Westerner into his or her animality. The vegetarian who is completely opposed to the consumption of flesh, on the contrary, wants to abolish the human and animality in the name of an extremely idealized representation of the animal. This thesis seems extreme in the contemporary context of environmental concern. But since Greek antiquity the Westerner has been plagued by the temptation to declare human exceptionalism. Given our defective memory, the recollection of the animality of human beings is in part metabolic. To accept eating meat is to acknowledge that there are no "free lunches" in this lowly world. That being alive consists in receiving and giving joy and suffering. That being alive means being harmed by other living beings and harming them in return. To believe that one can live and occupy a position of innocence is pure fantasy. In contrast, eating meat should be seen as a way of reaffirming one's animality in terms of what constitutes us fundamentally as animals. The human being is in fact an omnivore who eats meat. This diet is not simply *nutritional*; it is also *metaphysical, spiritual, and ethical.*

At the same time, the carnivore can limit his consumption of meat. It is also possible to assert a closer proximity to the animal by seeking to merge with it rather than by limiting one's ambition to the desire to live in peace with animals.

Before entering into the heart of the matter, I would like to point out that paradoxically I feel much closer to the majority of vegetarians I know than to the majority of carnivores with whom I have become acquainted. Thus, this essay is certainly not a book *against* vegetarians but rather against the most fundamentalist of them. It has never been a trivial matter for me to eat meat; instead I fully acknowledge its significance. Along with the majority of vegetarians, I think that what we eat is constitutive of what we are. But our conclusions from this common conviction differ considerably. I eat meat, and I want to continue to do so for reasons that are very close to the reasons why vegetarians do *not* want to eat it; there is almost an exact symmetry here.

In our time, the defender of animals and the vegetarian are assumed to walk hand in hand. Defending animals and eating them are two attitudes customarily seen as contradictory. The situation is more complex than that. In particular, there is an entire intellectual tradition of carnivores that has consistently and sincerely defended animals and nature. Take, for example, Aldo Leopold, one of the fathers of American environmentalism, or Paul Shepard, one of the principal theorists of the necessary relations between human beings and other animals. It is in this intellectual space, still little known in France, that I situate the present book.

APPETIZER

How Does One
Recognize an
Ethical Vegetarian?

A VEGETARIAN IS A HUMAN BEING who *prefers* to eat only plants (vegetables and fruits), even though she possesses metabolically, physically, and financially the capacity to eat meat. Metabolically, she can digest meat, provided that it is available. Someone who does not eat meat because it would make her sick is not really considered a vegetarian. By the same token, an inhabitant of a large Western city who does not have enough money to eat meat cannot be considered a vegetarian.[1] A vegetarian is one who makes a *positive* choice (to eat only plants, fruits, and vegetables—and of course mushrooms) or a *negative* one (not to eat meat) among other possible choices.

In this chapter, I first attempt to characterize the vegetarian position and then subject it to critique from the carnivorous point of view. The vegetarian will not necessarily agree with my way of characterizing his position, but we need not always *characterize the vegetarian from the point of view of a vegetarian.*

Who Are Vegetarians?

At the risk of being shocking, I would say that the term *preference* used earlier needs to be taken at face value. A preference is something I choose even though other possibilities are open to me. There can be more than one reason for the choice I make. The reasons offered by vegetarians in order to adopt a dietary regime without meat are sometimes mutually incompatible. Thus, many vegetarians base their choice on dietary reasons: they believe (whether they are right or wrong is not at issue here) that it is better for one's health not to eat meat. Other vegetarians adopt this practice for aesthetic reasons (they simply do not like the taste of meat) or psychological ones (they have had a traumatic experience that prevents them from returning to meat as a source of nutrition). Finally, an increasing number of vegetarians abstain from eating meat for ethical reasons. They believe that such conduct is immoral or has consequences that are regrettable, indeed unacceptable, in the short to long run. In 1989, Paul Amato and Sonia Partridge reported that around nine million people in the United States were vegetarians, which was about 4 percent of the population. Sixty-seven percent of them were vegetarians on grounds of protest against the animal suffering caused by meat consumption; 5 percent cited problems of world hunger, and 38 percent cited a desire to promote personal health.[2]

The following pages are devoted exclusively to "ethical vegetarians," those in the third category just outlined. The ethical vegetarian refuses to eat meat because it is necessary to subject a sentient being to suffering and death in order to eat it. The ethical vegetarian often appeals to a right possessed by the animal, a right that started to be conceptualized in the 1970s, although the foundational text that is constantly invoked in this connection is a text by Jeremy Bentham that dates from 1789. Defenders of animal rights generally adopt (although not always) a pointedly Anglo-Saxon utilitarian perspective according to which animals have interests. As sentient and intelligent beings, animals have in particular the right not to be killed in order to be eaten. There is another argument that is more empirical and cognitive. Animals indisputably possess an intelligence that is incompatible with being treated as simple means or as things. Given their cognitive and emotional capacities, they have the right not to be eaten by human beings for the same reasons that a human being has the right not to be eaten by another human. The most extreme militants advocate an even more radical position according to which all animal products, such as eggs and milk, not to mention leather and fur, must be proscribed. These individuals are the vegans. Finally, a group that is small yet extremely active in Anglo-Saxon countries links feminism and vegetarian practices. Without a doubt, it is Carol J. Adams who has done the most work to establish this position in a famous book that has been widely commented on: *The Sexual Politics of Meat*.[3] She argues in particular that meat constitutes an important figure of masculine oppression; thus, the animal to be eaten is reduced to steak for the same reasons that and according to similar ideological procedures as the woman as object is reduced to a man's sexual desire.

HORS
D'OEUVRE

A Short History of
Vegetarian Practices

A VERY QUICK HISTORY OF VEGETARIAN practices is imperative. It is not without value to know how vegetarians arrived at their convictions. Nor is it a trivial matter to demonstrate that the vegetarian position, far from being monolithic, has a complexity greater than the majority of vegetarians believe. There are few histories of vegetarian movements, and some of them are more interesting than others. The one that I consider the best and that has given me the greatest inspiration for the pages that follow is the one published by Colin Spencer in 1993.[1]

Pythagoras and the Rejection of Cannibalism

If Pythagoras is frequently cited as a foundational figure by vegetarians possessing some erudition, this lineage is problematic. Egypt does have its vegetarians, and Zoroaster had already advocated abstention from meat. To justify his restrictive diet, Pythagoras offers two arguments. The first appeals to the idea of an *active* vegetarian diet. A human being's nutrition should be vegetarian because eating plants is most worthy. For Pythagoras, who in Babylon was initiated into practices including the consumption of psychoactive drugs from plants originating from Persia, vegetarian food with aromatic spices is the food of the gods, and human beings are to emulate the gods.

The second argument might seem to be closer to the one brandished by contemporary vegetarians, but this is only an appearance. Pythagoras refuses to kill animals because of his belief in metempsychosis. The reincarnations that take place between species make it necessary to recognize in each animal a potential cousin whom it is indecent to eat. Thus, it is not the refusal to kill animals that constitutes the basis of Pythagoras's approach but rather the refusal to engage in cannibalism. One ought not eat animals because each of them is potentially a reincarnated human being.

The prohibition on consuming meat is not the only restriction specified by Pythagoras: one must also abstain from eating beans. Why? The reason is far from clear. In his book *The Gardens of Adonis*, the Hellenist Marcel Détienne focuses on Pythagoras's "sacred words" and explains that the bean is the only plant whose stalk lacks nodes, which makes it a privileged means of communication between the living and the dead as well as between humans and the gods.[2] For the Pythagoreans, eating beans is equivalent to an act of cannibalism. Thus, their vegetarianism is rooted fundamentally in a religious practice; it is based on the privileged status accorded to plants and involves a refusal to eat meat not in order to avoid making animals suffer or to accord them respect but in order to avoid cannibalistic or semicannibalistic practices unworthy of human beings. In Pythagoras's view, however, the only difference between human beings and other animals is that the latter have only an *inner language*, whereas the former have an *exterior language* as well—even though the Neoplatonist philosopher Iamblichus takes a different approach: abstaining from meat leads one to become a devotee of peace.

Plutarch's Psychological Vegetarianism

Plato was profoundly inspired by Pythagorean doctrines such as the immortality of the soul, but he was never a vegetarian, even though many Neoplatonists were; among them, Porphyry is the best known. Nor was Aristotle a vegetarian in spite of the fact that he asserted an equivalence (one considered rather doubtful nowadays) between slaves and animals. In ancient thought, Plutarch had very little influence. An atypical vegetarian, he was the first Greek not to link his vegetarian practice to the immortality of a soul. In his writings, Plutarch instead justifies his refusal to eat meat by citing the repugnance inspired in him by a killed and dismembered animal. In addition, he is persuaded that eating meat makes human beings aggressive. In other words, his vegetarianism is more psychological than ethical or religious. Plutarch also explores at length the origins of humanity's consumption of meat. For him, the human being is a special kind of carnivore compared with other animals: a carnivore not by nature but rather by culture and even by a cultural perversion.

Tertullian's Ascetic Vegetarianism

From the moment the emperor Constantine makes Christianity the state religion in 313, Christian convictions become influential and come to establish a monopoly. For Christians, human beings represent the dominant species. Neither equality nor justice nor compassion are owed to animals. Eating meat is part of the way one leads one's life so as to honor God. Meat is a gift from God that improves the quality of human beings' lives. To refrain from eating it would almost constitute blasphemy inasmuch as doing so would amount to refusing what God has given us so generously. And yet the Gnostic Dead Sea Scrolls paint a picture of a different Jesus, one linked to vegetarian sects. Moreover, it is not the case that all Christians became more or less savage carnivores. Tertullian (160–240 CE), for example, expresses outrage at Christians who proffer the idea that Christ and the apostles would have permitted the consumption of meat. He even writes a book on this subject. This may be the first time that eating meat is associated with carnal desire and luxury.

The Manichaeans' Refusal of Flesh

The Manichaeans refuse to eat meat for a completely different reason. For them, it is not, as it is for the Pythagoreans, a *positive reason* that amounts to respecting another living creature endowed with a soul. Instead, it is a *negative reason* based on fear, suspicion, and disgust. To the extent that all material things are bad, meat belongs to the realm of evil. Consuming it can only encumber the soul and hinder it in its flight toward God.

The Cathars, who belong to the Manichaean lineage, also believe that all flesh is monstrous inasmuch as it is born of copulation and thus is impure. Or at least this is what they claimed in public. For Eckbert von Schönau, who between 1163 and 1167 wrote a sermon directed against the Cathars, the real reason is even worse: all flesh is a work of evil, and seeking it as a source of nutrition is to be avoided, even in situations of grave necessity. Christian society, which combats the Manichaeans as well as the Cathars and other heretical vegetarians, counts among its numbers those monks and saints who abstain from eating meat. Nonetheless, this austere diet is considered above all a way of approaching God.

Dissident Voices

Later, in the Renaissance, some dissident voices make themselves heard in Christianity in an even more insistent manner. Erasmus (1466–1536) in particular paints a very cutting portrait of hunters and their ritual killings in *Praise of Folly*. But it is his friend Thomas More who in *Utopia* presents the strongest condemnation of the hunting and murder of wild animals. The English philosopher is also the first to note that the raising of flocks and herds requires a very large quantity of land. Nonetheless, even if a number of thinkers of the time, including Montaigne, reconsider the status of the animal, very few genuinely pursue the path of vegetarianism. Leonardo da Vinci is one of these exceptions. He speaks of the mouth as "a tomb for all the animals" and refuses to eat meat, but without really giving any reasons, in contrast with the esoteric thinker Jakob Böhme, who will justify his vegetarian dietary choices by arguing that killing an animal in order to eat it erects a wall between his soul and God.

Being Vegetarian During the Time of Cartesian Regression

Pierre Gassendi is known for being a fierce opponent of Cartesianism. In his objections to Descartes's *Meditations*, he harshly attacks the doctrine of the animal–machine by showing that animals experience emotions and that the criterion of language for distinguishing human beings from animals is just plain stupid. But he also disputes the idea that human beings need to eat meat. Gassendi tells his friend Van Helmont, who maintains that human beings are intrinsically carnivores, that humans' teeth are closer to those of herbivores, which possess teeth that fit together in a regular way, than they are to the teeth of carnivores. Citing Plutarch, he adds that human beings, lacking organs and abilities for killing other animals with their bare hands, have no reason to persist in their desire to consume them. And defenders of animals are not always those one might expect. Thus, Bossuet, Bishop of Meaux, likens killing animals to an act of war! But at that time it is really in England that vegetarian ethics starts to flourish.

English Vegetarians in the Seventeenth and Eighteenth Centuries

The major figure among English vegetarians during this time is without a doubt Thomas Tryon, who converted to this dietary regime after having discovered the works of Jakob Böhme in 1657. His influence extends as far as Percy Shelley, and there is no question that he is the author of the first book of vegetarian recipes, *Bill of Fare of Seventy-Five Noble Dishes of Excellent Food* (1691).

Tryon is by no means isolated. He shares his vegetarian convictions with some eminent minds of his time, in particular John Ray, fellow of the Royal Society and a naturalist and botanist of the first order, as well as John Gray and Alexander Pope.

At the same time, other influential figures hold more traditional carnivorous positions. In 1653, Henry More explains that cattle breeding is the best means for providing fresh meat. If this practice inspires few criticisms, vivisection, which is just beginning to be developed, is met with more violent and sustained objections. Finally, the first treatise on the rights of animals appears in 1776 under the pen of the Reverend Humphrey Primatt: *A Dissertation on the Duty of Mercy and Sin of Cruelty to Brute Animals.*

Vegetarian Societies

It is in 1847 that the *Pythagorean* diet officially becomes *vegetarian* in the course of a meeting at the Northwood Villa in Ramsgate, an infirmary dedicated to the treatment of illnesses with water; the infirmary is directed by William Horsell, who will be present at the inception of the Vegetarian Society. Horsell is very much influenced by the work of the German chemist Justus Liebig, who asserts that there is no difference between animal and vegetable protein and demonstrates that plants constitute the primary source of protein. This insight is considered to be the first scientific validation of vegetarian doctrines. The Ramsgate meeting gathers together biblical Christians but also members of the Alcott House Concordium, a very strict educational college that preaches a natural life that eschews wool and requires cold baths at five o'clock in the morning, raw food, and celibacy. In 1850, William Metcalfe (an American disciple of Emanuel Swedenborg, who considers meat eating to be a sign of our fall) founds the American Vegetarian Society.

At this time, the defense of the vegetarian position becomes focused essentially on dietary health. Meat is assumed to render its consumers aggressive and brutal, whereas vegetarian nutrition is supposed to guarantee the greatest longevity. Very much a minority movement, English vegetarianism benefits greatly from the huge change in the sensibilities of the English regarding slaughterhouses. In addition, some horrible stories regarding the savagery inspired by meat eating helps to make the refusal to eat meat appealing. Nonetheless, the number of vegetarians fluctuates greatly in the course of the nineteenth century. At the end of the century, the emergence of a middle class permits vegetarianism to gain new momentum. Socialism, pastoralism, and the ideal of a simple life play a role in this renewal.

Figures in the Vegetarian Movement in the Nineteenth and Twentieth Centuries

George Bernard Shaw's vegetarian diet contributes greatly to the visibility of the movement, but the English playwright is by no means the sole major figure in the vegetarian movement at the turn of the twentieth century. Richard Wagner presents his vegetarian theories in a series of essays published between 1880 and

1883, the year of his death. The German composer, who requires his entourage to be vegetarian, is forced by his poor health to eat meat, and he hates it. If one believes his daughter-in-law, Winifred Wagner, he would have wanted to be a vegetarian for purely ethical reasons, like Tolstoy or Gandhi. At the same time, influential writers such as George Orwell and G. K. Chesterton (who in other respects were completely or almost completely opposed to one another) had nothing but mistrust for vegetarians. Vegetarian convictions develop in the 1930s along with the fashion for fresh air, sunbathing, nudism, and the discovery of the health benefits of fruits and vegetables. The American Gayelord Hauser and the Swiss Maximilian Oskar Bircher-Benner open vegetarian clinics. In 1928, Nina Hosali founds the Nature Cure Clinic. Ideas already found in Mani, the founding father of Manichaeanism, or in the Gnostics acquire a new youth. Sir John Boyd Orr is the first to link health and dietary regime. Nonetheless, it would not be until 1944 that the Vegan Society would be created in Leicester. Curiously, postwar literature dispenses with the idea that a vegetarian diet makes men kind and favors peace. The vegetarian regime attributed to Hitler is perhaps not out of place here.

Counterculture and Animal Rights at the End of the Twentieth Century

In the course of the second half of the twentieth century, the status of vegetarians changes considerably under the influence of the counterculture and some new ecological movements. The expression *animal rights* is born in 1965 under the pen of Brigid Brophy, who uses it as the title of an article published in the Sunday *Times*, by analogy to the title of Thomas Paine's book *The Rights of Man* (1791). *The Findhorn Garden* by Peter and Eileen Caddy is a comparable chronicle of the new communitarian adventures of the time. Completely vegetarian, the community that establishes itself along with the two authors on the Moray Firth grows flowers and giant vegetables in cooperation with the spirits of nature. Eileen Caddy writes that members of the community derive their nutrition from "subtle energies" found in plants, absorbing the light that is the starting point for the growth of vegetables and fruits.

In the 1960s, being a vegetarian becomes very popular in Great Britain. In 1968, there are sixteen vegetarian restaurants in London and eighteen in the entire rest of the country. In 1978, there are fifty-two in London and eighty throughout Great Britain. From the counterculture emerges the idea that the human being is a user of the planet and ought to exercise care. In the 1970s, the notion of "pure food" without pesticides or chemical additives begins to spread. Later, the revelation of the horrors of industrial breeding contributes to the conversion of many people to a vegetarian diet. During the 1990s, for example, in Great Britain several thousand people join the ranks of vegetarians every week. These new adherents come not only from the middle class but also from the working class. Moreover, nutritionists are finding more and more good reasons to adopt a vegetarian diet. In this connection, the National Advisory Committee on Nutritional Education publishes a report (that the British government attempts to suppress) emphasizing that a proper diet is low in saturated fat (which is present above all in animals), low in salt and sugar, but rich in fiber, which is all but absent in meat.

FIRST COURSE

Some (Good) Reasons *Not*
to Become an
Ethical Vegetarian

IN THE CASE FOR VEGETARIANISM: *Philosophy for a Small Planet*, published in 1996, the American philosopher John Lawrence Hill analyzes the vegetarian position with an eye toward defending it against carnivores' objections.[1] This text offers an interesting point of departure for examining the baroque reasoning that characterizes the vegetarian position.

Hill challenges the argument that the domestic animals that provide meat for our societies would be destined to disappear if a universal vegetarian regime were implemented. It is indisputable that many animals, those raised exclusively for consumption, would not be born if we all were vegetarians. However, Hill challenges the argument in a manner that is not only disappointing but downright surprising: he concludes that by analogy one would now have to be willing to enslave children inasmuch as they would not exist if we did not do so. Does advocating the existence of a certain *biodiversity*, artificial though it may be, require being a slavist? And wouldn't it be simpler and more effective to respond that there is no evidence that there would be many fewer domestic animals if they were no longer eaten? Hill is more convincing when he maintains that existence is positive in itself, but he still lacks the ecological and patrimonial basis of the argumentation of the carnivore, who appeals not to the number of animals but to their diversity.

Hill goes completely awry when he asks why the human being should be the only sacred animal from a dietary point of view, for in fact this objection is a double-edged sword. A consistent carnivore, like the ethical vegetarian, could call this exception into question, but the carnivore would do so by proposing that one *also* eat humans. The carnivore could conclude that the "lack of things to eat" following from this questionable prohibition on meat eating would entail the squandering of a large proportion of our nutritional resources and that doing so would be for moral and sentimental reasons that are a little ridiculous. Hill is not convincing when he asks whether the brief life of a calf in circumstances of industrial farming is preferable to never having been born. Are meat eating and industrial farming as closely allied as he thinks?

The author becomes rather amusing when he states without hesitation that *more* deer could live if we stopped using the earth as pasture land to feed the animals we eat. However much the vegetarian may deny it, he or she is permanently haunted by the Bambi syndrome. Hill rightly emphasizes that there are some difficulties involved in justifying the consumption of meat on the grounds that this is what the animal itself prefers, but he neglects to add that this argument can be completely turned around. Can one say, for example, that the animal prefers not to die?

Challenging some carnivores' assertion that eating meat and killing other animals are part of human nature is more interesting. It is not necessarily a matter of arguing that the taste of meat is a physiological inheritance from our past. Eating meat is a correlate of our physiological constitution. It is easy for Hill to dispute the concrete proof offered by carnivores in support of this thesis. But here again his argument can be turned around and thus has little force. For why not dispute this proof on the same grounds as those marshaled by Hill against the carnivores? In any case, archaeological or historical demonstrations are difficult to carry out. Killing and being killed are part of nature, and being opposed to them seems somewhat laughable. Hill sidesteps this objection by means of an unconvincing pirouette: the fact that everything must die, he says, does not mean that human beings have the right to kill! He relies on the distinction made by some philosophers between *killing* and *allowing to die*. But a somewhat malicious carnivore might respond that she herself, like the vast majority of Western carnivores, has not killed a single animal and that in fact she is less an active predator than a vulture who contents herself with eating meat that she finds already dead at the butcher shop.

The clearest implication of Hill's argumentation is something else. It is to be found in Hill's certitude, which he never calls into question, that there is only one good way to interact with other animals, one way that poses no problems, leaves no residue, inspires no hesitation, and leads to no aporia: not eating them. In brief, Hill believes that the vegetarian position has nothing but advantages and no gray areas.

The Vegetarian's Ethical Miracle

Clearly evident in Hill's plea is a basic characteristic of vegetarian argumentation that until now has not been given much emphasis: the vegetarian position is always presented as having no costs and immense advantages. Such an "ethical miracle" can only make critical minds suspicious. Neither God nor evolution has accustomed us to such gifts. In real life, roses always have thorns. An examination of vegetarian doctrines that employs some critical distance reveals a more complex situation.

In this connection, one can cite several major problems with the vegetarian position. In it one finds above all a hierarchy of living beings that entails a political apartheid between human beings and other animals. This apartheid leads to a rehabilitation of human exceptionalism and the removal of human beings from the state of animality. It leads further to a deadly dimension of vegetarian ethics, which can only seek to eradicate animality itself. It finally leads to a refusal to acknowledge the place of cruelty in the world and to the assertion of a place of innocence for human beings that leads them to want to remake the world in accordance with their unrealistic aspirations. The ethical vegetarian's standpoint is also surprising in that it makes no place for a conflict of interests among living beings and is unable to comprehend any kind of harmony other than that of a moral equilibrium in the space of the living. The central paradox of ethical vegetarianism follows: What are carnivores supposed to do when their interests differ from those of their prey?

Plants, Too, Are Sentient Beings

At the heart of the vegetarian position is a hierarchy of living beings. The vegetarian relies in particular on a radical distinction between animals, which are the object of all the vegetarian's attention, and plants, which are essentially instrumentalized. The vegetarian assumes that eating plants involves neither killing nor the infliction of suffering. But plants are living beings that die. Why should it be any more legitimate to kill a plant than an animal? J. B. S. Haldane characterized the vegetarian as someone who does not hear the cries of the carrot he consumes. Why would it be more ethical to make a carrot suffer than a hare? Such a question will make more than one reader smile but cannot be casually brushed aside. In fact, it is quite subversive. The argument that the carrot suffers less than the hare is flawed in that it relies on the very hierarchy of levels of suffering that the ethical vegetarian rejects. Typically, the ethical vegetarian sincerely believes that the plants he consumes in such good conscience do not suffer and have no interests of their own, but his conviction is neither as rational nor as empirically grounded as he supposes.

That plants have a certain sentience is an idea widely held in most world cultures, and it is given particular credibility in shamanic cultures. In the West, this conviction has existed at least since Goethe. More and more research today explores this intriguing phenomenon, and the work of the botanist Anthony Trewavas of the University of Edinburgh plays a major role. In his book *Intelligence in Nature: An Inquiry Into Knowledge*, the anthropologist Jeremy Narby, who has undertaken an interdisciplinary investigation of intelligence, describes his encounter with the Scottish botanist.[2] For the specialist in shamanism of the Amazon, the intelligence of plants has always been an important question. In 2003, Trewavas described the *behavior* of Andean palms

(*Socratea exorrhiza*), showing how this tree turns toward the light by adjusting its roots and tries to displace its competitors so as to occupy locations with the greatest amount of sun. This activity lasts for months. Trewavas believes that plants have intentions, make decisions, and evaluate complex aspects of their environments. The study of ground ivy in a controlled environment in which nutrients are unequally distributed is just as interesting in this connection. This plant localizes resources by rapidly extending its roots into locations rich in nutrients. Without stopping, the roots extend through the barren soil so as to reach the more fertile portions as quickly as possible. From these observations, Trewavas concludes that an individual plant possesses the capacity to alter its morphology and transform the structure of its branches in order to adapt to its environment. Plants may not think, but they do make calculations and react appropriately to the problems they encounter.

The Scottish botanist has also studied dodder (*Cuscuta*) in this connection. It proceeds by wrapping itself around other species to evaluate their nutritive value. Within an hour, the dodder "decides" whether it is going to exploit its host or should look elsewhere. For Trewavas, the dodder makes an "active choice": if it remains, it will have to wait several days before it can avail itself of the nutrients available from the plant it is parasitizing, but it *anticipates* the potential riches in its environment when it grows a variable number of coils.

In 1990, Trewavas and his colleagues introduced a protein into tobacco plants that makes them glisten when the level of calcium increases in the interior of their cells. According to Trewavas, this change in the concentration of calcium in the cells is one of the principal means by which plants perceive external events. "Elevating calcium ion transduction constituents," he writes, "is analogous to increasing the numbers of connections in a neural network."[3] From this observation, he concludes that the resulting increase in the flow of information amounts to a sort of cellular apprenticeship and thus a sort of cellular intelligence. Every touch immediately causes tobacco to react. Human neurons produce more calcium when they transmit information. Plants learn, remember, and make decisions even though they lack a brain. In fact, they act *like* a brain.

Botanists confirm what gardeners and shamans have always known: plants are genuine living beings. This research has naturally inspired numerous debates in the scientific community. The controversy has focused in particular on the question whether the criteria employed by the Scottish botanist really showed that at least some plants can be considered intelligent. Such questions are entirely understandable. Nonetheless, the upshot of these investigations is absolutely clear: like all other living beings, plants have interests and actively pursue them. They may not possess an intelligence comparable to that of mammals, but to continue to view them as if they were simple objects at the disposal of human beings is not a defensible option. Narby concludes his chapter on plant intelligence with a powerful thought experiment: "I tried to find my way into the framework of plant time, but my thoughts continued to pass at animal speed. An image came to my mind:

that of Trewavas seated in a chair, motionless, engaged in thinking about plants. He acted like a plant in order to understand plants, and he attributed intelligence to them. Like a shaman, he identified with nature in the name of knowledge. His eyes glimmered."[4]

The Vegetarian's Hierarchy of Beings

In supposing that it is less harmful to consume vegetables than to eat animals, the vegetarian assumes that a vegetable, an earthworm, or the insect that she kills when she cultivates her garden is less important than a cow. Here it is reasonable to ask the vegetarian why she surreptitiously reintroduces the kind of *hierarchy of beings* that she rejects elsewhere. Some individuals, such as Joanne Elizabeth Lauck, are beginning to raise their voices in protest of the scant importance accorded to insects. If a cow is more intelligent (or more sentient) than an earthworm (which is by no means obvious), then is the vegetarian prepared to eat cows that are *sufficiently* insensitive and ultimately to transform them by means of biotechnology into *completely* insensitive animals in order to make consumption of them morally permissible?

This cognitive criterion, which has become so prevalent among Westerners in the twenty-first century, is far from being universally accepted. Without a doubt, a Hindu would rather kill a chimpanzee than a cow, even if the cow is less intelligent than the primate. Why should the Hindu's value system be less worthy of consideration than the Westerner's?

A Gradualist Ethics

Most ethical vegetarians, however, reject a completely clear-cut conception of good and evil. Like the vast majority of people, they believe that the *degree of severity* is important. Stealing is reprehensible, but stealing a dollar is less serious than stealing a thousand; stealing a wallet that we find on the ground is less serious than physically assaulting the owner of the wallet in order to get it; and such a physical assault is less serious than killing the owner of the wallet. So why should killing an animal *always* be reprehensible? In any case, no ethical vegetarian, unless he is a crazed lunatic, is prepared to send someone to prison for killing a mosquito or a cockroach. In other words, he accepts more or less implicitly the proposition that killing a mosquito or a cockroach is different than killing a cow. It is against this background that we need to discuss the difference between killing a cow and killing a human being.

Many vegetarians brandish the notion of antispeciesism in support of their desire not to kill animals. For the antispeciesist, it is not acceptable to privilege the members of one's own species to the detriment of members of other species. The term *speciesism*, introduced in 1970 by Richard Ryder and taken up again by Peter Singer in 1975, is modeled on the notion of racism. But does that make the term meaningful? This question is far from being settled. Consider: cannibalism is quite rare among animals and nonexistent among large carnivores. Are we to consider panthers speciesists because they refuse to eat one of their conspecifics?

Then why should human beings be considered speciesists if they are willing to kill a cow but not a human being in order to eat? Or, to put the point more precisely, why would they be *more* speciesist than a panther? It is clear to me that being willing to act in the same way as all predatory species is the only truly antispeciesist position inasmuch as I recognize myself to be a member of a community of animals and do not have any pretention to elevate myself above other species. Thus, paradoxically, a certain form of speciesism is the only way not to be speciesist—*being speciesist just as all other animals are.*

Do I harm an animal if I kill and eat it? Does it benefit from being killed and eaten by a predator other than a human being? Is what is most important for this animal to live longer as well as it can, or is it something else altogether? A sociobiologist such as Richard Dawkins would have a very different opinion on this matter than a vegetarian. Within the framework of his strict interpretation of evolution, he would maintain that every animal's primary interest is to reproduce as prolifically as possible. And from this standpoint, a balanced ethical position would not entail refraining from eating a cow but instead would entail affording the cow an adequate opportunity to reproduce before eating it.

At the species level, predation has played a major evolutionary role; the only way to consider it bad a priori would be to extend the sphere of morality beyond the boundaries within which it makes sense. In this connection, it is worth noting that some animals exist precisely *because* they are prey—for example, European bison, which have survived on Polish game preserves—but this argument is not as strong as those who invoke it would have us believe (we can discuss the numbers and their relative importance), and in any case that is not the argument to which I am appealing here. I simply want to stress that the vegetarian's fundamental postulate that the animal's good consists in never being hunted or eaten is less obvious than the vegetarian suggests.

The Central Paradox of Vegetarian Ethics

Thus, it is the vegetarian rather than the carnivore who is speciesist. This speciesism is clear in what might be called "the central paradox of vegetarian ethics." One of the vegetarian's primary convictions is that it is good not to make animals suffer. Now, one way suffering can occur is by means of a suppression of pleasure. Given that the carnivore is an animal that derives a great deal of pleasure from eating meat, to prevent him or her from doing so amounts to inflicting a certain amount of suffering on him or her. So to force the carnivore to be an ethical vegetarian is actually antivegetarian.

Naturally, the vegetarian can claim that this displeasure is not suffering, but in doing so she holds herself out to be a universal judge and is overstepping her proper role. She may also claim that the suffering of a carnivore deprived of meat is less important than that of a cow that gets eaten, but this suggestion is completely gratuitous and so openly opportunistic as to make one smile. From the kind of utilitarian standpoint defended by ethical vegetarians such as Peter Singer, the question arises why the animal's pleasure in not being eaten should be considered superior to the pleasure I experience from eating it. There is no reason to suppose that such conflicting interests can be resolved straightforwardly. It will be necessary to return to this point a little later.

Denying in the case of human beings a need that is fundamental to all living beings is not without precedent. At least since antiquity and undoubtedly even before it, there have been spiritual or moral movements that have considered to be bad certain things prevailing among animals that the vast majority of human beings have always considered to be good. Sexuality, the enjoyment of food, and art have regularly been summoned before the tribunals of despoiled virtue and religious fundamentalism. To seek to deny to humanity, under various moral pretexts, forms of behavior present in all animals is a common feature of all religious movements in the history of humankind, and this fact is highly problematic.

Pleasure is clearly an essential dimension of meat eating. The vegetarian claims that it is not necessary to eat meat in order to enjoy a delicious meal and that it is possible to prepare excellent vegetarian cuisine. The fact that he is right about this latter point has no bearing on the somewhat specious character of his reasoning. People who are opposed to alcohol say that a glass of milk or juice provides just as much pleasure as a glass of high-quality wine, but this simply is not true for anyone who loves wine and hates milk! Even if drinking a glass of milk may be quite pleasant for some people, a wine enthusiast is not going to get the same kind of pleasure from doing so.

But the pleasure derived from eating meat would be tainted to the extent that it is predicated on the other's suffering. Sadism is undoubtedly a perverse pleasure, but there is a bit of sadism in the reasoning that would deny the pleasure of eating meat. The fact that some people take pleasure in the suffering of others does not mean that everyone who makes some others suffer is a sadist.

Thus, the vegetarian is a very special kind of speciesist in that he is prepared to deny to members of his own species what he is prepared to grant to all the members of all other species: the ability to pursue their own interests.

Knowing Better Than the Animal What Is in Its Interest

The notion of interests is an extremely delicate matter, and some of the most extreme (or most consistent) vegetarians do not hesitate to attribute some rather questionable interests to animals. Steve Sapontzis, for example, is prepared to transform the biology of predatory animals so as to turn them into herbivores or frugivores.

The radical vegetarian who would like to turn foxes into vegetarians believes that humans can place themselves above evolution and all other species. Such a person believes that meat eating is immoral and ought to be spurned and that she is entitled to make a moral judgment about everyone's dietary regime. She endeavors to legislate human diet in the name of other animals even though they have asked nothing of her.

In order to preclude an objection that will no doubt be made here, I would like to point out that refusing to make a moral judgment about what a species eats does not mean that evolution is in fact the only value that matters (as in the most cursory accounts of social Darwinism or evolutionary psychology); that would be all too simplistic.

The Claim of Human Exceptionalism

The position taken up by the ethical vegetarian regarding the split between human and animal is paradoxically very close to that of the humanist. The humanist believes that there is a fundamental ontological barrier between human and animal and that animals may be instrumentalized without any danger of doing anything morally inappropriate. In contrast with the European humanist, the vegetarian does not conclude from this that she may treat animals any way she likes; she instead reasserts in a novel form the doctrine of human uniqueness by refusing to let herself become intoxicated by the animal and by assuming that the metabolic relationships between human and animal should be reduced to a minimum, if not completely suppressed. Here eating meat can be viewed as a form of the animalization of the human being, animal flesh becoming transformed into human flesh.

This idea of human beings becoming intoxicated by the animal is clearly discussed by Florence Burgat in her book *Liberté et inquiétude de la vie animale* (The freedom and restlessness of animal life). In a passionate chapter on xenografts, Burgat quotes professor Pierre Cüer, a specialist in these transplant procedures, as stating that "reassuring the patient who will receive the transplant that he will remain human" is one of the two ethical obligations that he owes to each of his patients.[5]

The vegetarian similarly eschews wildness by rejecting anything that would introduce a wild element; that is, she rejects any possibility of becoming metabolically transformed by a living being of another species. In this manner, she rehabilitates the doctrine of human exceptionalism: she assumes that she is the sole carnivorous (or potentially carnivorous) animal who ought to place herself above her omnivorous animal condition and that this is to be achieved by distancing herself from one of the central characteristics of that condition—preying on other animals.

To this extent, the vegetarian's position appears to be fundamentally one of apartheid, even if the vegetarian does not acknowledge it to be so. This position is also highly original in the history of Western thought: however friendly the animal may be, it ought to be kept at a distance.

Thus, the ethical vegetarian reasserts human exceptionalism, although she would deny this and go so far as to claim that she is fighting for the recognition of the other as an equal. At first blush, the situation seems a bit paradoxical, but it can ultimately be given a clear explanation. The vegetarian believes that human beings constitute a *moral exception* who ought to subject themselves to novel moral prohibitions with regard to other living beings. On this view, the vegetarian is the sole moral living being; this claim distinguishes the vegetarian ipso facto from all other animals and even gives the vegetarian the right to modify animals biologically. In this connection, it is worth considering whether human beings can assert as a positive universal principle what are really nothing more than forms of conduct in which they alone are capable of engaging.

The vegetarian will naturally object that such a position is really that of the social Darwinists, with whom he refuses to be identified. This objection is weak. It is true that the social Darwinists advocated a fanciful conception of life, but they sought to control the social dynamics of power, not any fundamental metabolic processes. Those who opposed social Darwinism challenged the proposition that lessons for the social life of humans can be learned from the social lives of animals. The vegetarian takes an entirely different tack, asserting on the contrary that moral lessons are to be learned by rejecting what amounts to a fundamental characteristic of all living beings. What sort of speciesist pride leads us to suppose that it is immoral for a living being to do what all other living beings do? Is not our aim in doing so to grant ourselves an exceptional status? The vegetarian would like to remove himself from the circle of life. He imagines that he can occupy a position in which he is no longer burdened by the *constraints of reciprocity* in life. To this extent, he ascribes to himself an extraterritoriality that is highly problematic. By means of this disruptive gesture, he separates himself radically from animality and seeks to separate animality from the living.

Conflicts of Interests

More generally, the vegetarian refuses to acknowledge that the real world is inherently a world of conflict and that the interests of different beings, far from being mutually compatible, tend to clash with one another. In what sense is a prey animal's interest in not being eaten superior to the predator's interest in eating its prey? In what sense is the cultural interest of a people such as the Inuit, whose collective identity is to a large extent based on meat eating, inferior to the biological interest of a seal in not being eaten? In other words, in what sense is the interest in life always superior to all other interests? The vegetarian refuses to grasp the fact that permanent conflicts of interest constitute a fundamental characteristic of the living.

The Posture of Innocence as Imposture

It is legitimate and even desirable for political institutions to try to introduce greater human justice into the social world: established institutions strengthen the weak and improve their lot. It is neither shocking nor unrealistic that the weak band together in order to eliminate strong individuals. In contrast, the endeavor to eliminate cruelty from the world altogether is shocking and unrealistic, for two reasons. First, because eliminating strong individuals who are hostile is cruel to those strong individuals who have become weak. And, second, because the belief that cruelty can be completely eradicated reflects a one-sided analysis of the situation. To see only advantages and no costs here is to subscribe to a fragmentary vision of the world.

In fact, a major point of disagreement between vegetarians and carnivores finds especially clear expression in relation to the question of cruelty. Cruelty plays a fundamental role in the vegetarian's argument inasmuch as the principal reason the vegetarian does not want to eat meat is that she does not want to kill animals or cause them to suffer. The vegetarian sees cruelty in purely negative terms; she believes that its complete eradication is a realistic goal that she ought to pursue actively. The carnivore, in contrast, considers such a pretention to be neither realistic nor desirable. To be fully animal we must openly acknowledge that life, even if we cannot place a price on it, is certainly not without its costs. In other words, when I eat animals, I accept the fact that my animality demands an inherent compromise rather than permit myself the luxury of supposing that I stand above animality and that I can detach myself morally from what amounts to a fundamental characteristic of my condition. Eating an animal amounts to sharing the burden of animality with other animals.

By being willing to eat animals, I acknowledge in particular and in an intimate manner that there are no "free lunches" in the world—that is, that one cannot want to be an animal and at the same time not want to be implicated in the cycles of life and death that are essential to being an animal. I kill in order to live, just like all other animals. The vegetarian succumbs to the illusion that all this can be easily avoided. She wants to believe that human beings can be an exception in the world by living in a completely self-sufficient manner, without ever killing or harming another living being. This seemingly sympathetic vision is utterly unrealistic and downright pathological in that it refuses to acknowledge the role that death and harm play in the dynamic of the living. When I refuse to kill in order to eat meat, I assume that such an activity is morally reprehensible even though a great many animals live by means of predation and we ourselves have survived in part because of hunting. Can practices that are so widespread and that have played such a significant role in the dynamic of species really be considered immoral?

The idea that there is evil in something so central to the processes constitutive of life is embarrassing. Of course, the vegetarian can maintain that the carnivorous nonhuman animal, in contrast with the human being, has no choice. This is yet another questionable claim, one that relies on incomplete reasoning. Species did have a "choice," at a particular moment, between becoming carnivores, omnivores, frugivores, or herbivores. Vegetarians are not the only ones to have made a choice. One will object that the vegetarian makes a personal or social choice, whereas a carnivorous species such as the tiger made a biological choice, a choice on the level of species that is not comparable. Such an objection is meaningful only if we attribute an extraordinary significance to the kind of choice that the human being makes, a significance predicated on the assumption that human beings stand at a distance from other animals and enjoy a primacy over them. The posture of innocence is fundamentally an ethical imposture.

Killing and Inflicting Suffering

The categorical rejection of cruelty and suffering is clearly reflected in the vegetarian's refusal to kill in order to eat. The complete eradication of cruelty and suffering is neither possible nor desirable. Refusing to kill would appear to be a more realistic goal. It at least deserves some consideration.

The vegetarian is a bit too rash in drawing a parallel between causing an animal to suffer and killing it. Wanting to minimize the suffering to which animals are subjected is a legitimate moral imperative. Refusing to kill an animal at all costs is much less of one. Death is a fundamental principle of life. Dying even constitutes a defining characteristic of the living. The vegetarian will clearly be troubled by this reasoning. He will even maintain that I am not hearing what he is saying—namely, that he does not want to abolish death but simply to allow animals to die in their own good time. But if I do not understand what the vegetarian is saying here, it is because what he is telling me simply cannot be heard. From the animal's point of view—and the animal's is the only one that counts in the ethical perspective that the vegetarian wants to adopt—does this difference make sense? Being killed can never be considered an ethical scandal for an animal. The belief that it can be is the product of a fundamental anthropomorphism. The claim that no animal wants to be eaten is either a meaningless commonplace or a plain falsehood. And even if this is not the case, neither would a plant "want" to be eaten. The truth is that no living being "wants" to die. Does this mean that it is always in its interest not to be killed? This may be the case if we give a weak meaning to the notion of interests, but, even so, as species become increasingly refined and complex under the pressure of predation, "personal" interests come into conflict with those of the species. And if we were to push this reasoning to the extreme, it would require us to prevent animals from killing other animals. And this in turn would require us once again to see human beings as having a special status at the heart of the living world.

Not Killing in Order to Eat

The vegetarian may concede that he is prepared to kill in order to protect himself (from bacteria or a mosquito) but not in order to eat because he has a choice to eat other things. But this objection is not obviously legitimate. Even agriculture destroys wild ecosystems and the animals living in them; it is pure fancy for vegetarians to believe that they have "clean stomachs" and that they can feed themselves without killing any animals or causing them to suffer. In order to be completely consistent, vegetarians would have to eat only what they harvest themselves because all agricultural activity destroys ecosystems in which animals live. In such a scenario, however, even if there were only a thousandth of the current human population on the earth, we would all certainly starve to death.

One might also suppose that to the extent that the problem consists in killing animals, we ought to devise ways of producing meat that do not involve killing. This idea is not as absurd as it might appear at first blush. The Australian artist Oron Catts and

43

the group SymbioticA at the University of Western Australia have succeeded in synthesizing frog steaks out of biopsied tissue. In 2003, their performance *Disembodied Cuisine* focused on a culture of frog skeletal muscle grown over biopolymer with the aim of making a product fit for human consumption. The biopsy was performed on a living animal that was able to continue to live while its steak grew alongside it. In the course of the performance, which took place in Nantes, frog cells were harvested by means of organogenesis in utero; in other words, the frog steak was cultivated from a frog that had not yet been born. In 2000, the first nonanimal steak grown by the artists—now housed in the Laboratory for Tissue Engineering and Organ Fabrication at Massachusetts General Hospital—was created from the skeletal muscles of a sheep and from a tissue culture in utero. The aim of this experimentation was to produce "meat without a victim"! Here one may pose the question posed by Oron Catts, Ionat Zurr, and Guy Ben-Ary: "Will the arrival of semi-living entities make our society more attentive to others, or will life become even more reified?"[6] Similarly, cloning an animal would enable us to eat it *without killing it completely*. This possibility, which will doubtless appear absurd to the vegetarian, shows convincingly that what is ultimately at stake is not necessarily what is given priority at the outset.

The Infinite Cruelty of a World Denuded of All Cruelty

The quest for a world devoid of suffering and cruelty is a priori appealing, but such a utopia is based on two false premises that need to be examined in depth. The first is that suffering is always something negative. The second is that such a world would be a good thing from the animal's standpoint.

In the first place, suffering has some fundamentally positive aspects. It permits a living being to feel its existence rather than simply passing through it. Human beings who do not suffer physically are in permanent danger in the world because they have no access to the sorts of psychophysiological stimuli that indicate that a limit has been reached. Feeling a burning sensation, for example, enables one to avoid being dangerously burned even before one realizes that the sensation is present.

Another paradoxically positive result of the existence of suffering and cruelty is that remarkable sentiments such as altruism and empathy have emerged from our sordid evolutionary history of blood and suffering. Here we might discuss numerous examples drawn from art, science, and personal experience more generally. They all demonstrate that a certain amount of cruelty is needed to confer substance on the world.

The fact that every animal seeks to minimize its own suffering by no means entails that suffering is devoid of meaning for it. In fact, the question we need to ask is what the meaning of a world devoid of suffering would be. There is no doubt that such a world would be not only untenable but also disturbingly sterile. Our reasoning is typically quite limited on such questions because we have a tendency to take our desires for reality; we do not take into account the costs associated with the actions we judge to be the most beneficial, as if goodness had no costs.

Thus, it might be possible to live in a world without cruelty, but such a world might be so colorless as to render life there infinitely cruel. This is exactly what J. Baird Callicott maintains when he states that it is impossible for an organism to attain a certain level of complexity without suffering and when he characterizes the viewpoint of those who seek a life without friction as the axiology of those who are disgusted by life.[7]

The Risk That Lies at the Heart of Living

A fundamental characteristic of living beings is to be exposed to and to take risks—that is, to consider suffering and pain to be less important than other interests. Thus, the vegetarian might admit, without becoming lost in any particularly tricky metaphysical considerations, that many millions of people prefer to become intoxicated on more or less illicit substances than to live as long as possible and that many millions of others prefer to live an interesting and risky life than a monotonous and placid one that may let them live longer but would be rather boring. If a vegetarian prefers to cultivate his carrot garden or explore inhospitable jungles in order to find rare fruits in them rather than drive race cars or scale mountain peaks, this is a matter of legitimate personal preferences that concern the vegetarian alone. There is no reason to turn this into a universal morality, and Candide is not a universal hero. Now, what holds true for human beings holds true for animals as well. There are many examples of this principle— for example, cats who wind up in desperate situations because they want to satisfy their curiosity, the (many) animals that consume psychotropic substances to the point of death, or those who are willing to place themselves in danger in order to supplant (or simply to remain) the one in charge.

If the question of animal suffering is a serious matter, it is altogether more complex than the vegetarian makes it appear when he refuses to admit that a certain amount of cruelty can have its place in the world. For the vegetarian, the world need not be a vale of tears; he considers it possible with a little good will, a great deal of work, and a few ad hoc laws to eliminate every trace of cruelty from the relationships that human beings have with other animals. Seen in these terms, the vegetarian's utopian endeavor can only generate support. But does goodness still exist when cruelty is completely eradicated? Such an ideal cannot be embraced by a living being, but only by a robot.

The Ethics of Cruelty

Especially relevant for understanding this optimistic and moralizing relationship that the vegetarian has to the world is the philosopher Clément Rosset's book *Le principe de cruauté* (The principle of cruelty), in which Rosset addresses the cruelty of reality and the strategies that have been employed to avoid it. Every attempt to minimize the cruelty of truth, to minimize the harshness of the real, he argues, has the unavoidable consequence of discrediting the most brilliant undertakings and the most worthy causes.[8]

Rosset sums up his "ethics of cruelty" by reference to two simple principles: the principle of sufficient reality and the principle of uncertainty. The first, which stipulates that reality need not be explained in terms of anything other than itself, is rejected by the majority of philosophers, with only a few very rare exceptions (Lucretius, Spinoza, Nietzsche, and Leibniz). And why is that? Because, writes Rosset, reality is cruel, painful, tragic, and ineluctable; indeed, it is doubly so inasmuch as not only is reality cruel, but this cruelty itself is entirely real. Confronted with this situation, human beings suffer from a dual handicap: their intellectual ability to become aware of the cruelty of the real and correlatively their psychological inability to endure it As Rosset puts it, not without some irony, the real is the enemy of the moral. He distinguishes philosophers according to the attitude they manifest toward this fact: thus, he opposes the philosopher-healers (sympathetic and ineffectual) to the philosopher-physicians (effective and ruthless).

The second principle, that of uncertainty, applies equally to the vegetarian. Human beings cannot endure uncertainty. The fanatic for a cause is fascinated by the seeming certainty of his or her cause. The refusal to accept the cruelty of the real and the endeavor to find a cause in which one can believe at all costs, even a cause that is opposed to the real itself, are an excellent characterization of the vegetarian.

In fact, at a deeper level, the consistent vegetarian turns out to be profoundly hostile to animal life. The only way truly to satisfy the vegetarian would be to suppress all animal life on earth, for this is the only solution that would effectively eradicate all suffering and all predation. Of course, most vegetarians deny in all good faith that they endorse such an endeavor. In a certain sense, this denial makes their situation look even worse in that they implicitly acknowledge the inanity and inconsistency of their approach. What, ultimately, is an ethical project that is to be only more or less realized?

Apropos of Evolution

The desire to live in an enchanted Walt Disney world devoid of suffering, cruelty, and irreducible conflicts of interests is a child's dream that those who have grown up a little bit have had to renounce. Theories of evolution are absolutely incompatible with Mickey Mouse's universe, even if we have abandoned once and for all the old Kiplingesque vision of the law of the jungle.

Darwin ultimately understood, although with great difficulty, how species evolve without a Grand Organizer by means of mutual selection. He recognized that all species are constantly in competition with one another and that the least-adaptive species (which are not necessarily the weakest) disappear to the advantage of the more adaptive ones. Thus, a principle of cruelty is at the heart of the Darwinian approach to the living, and Darwin has been roundly reproached for it because the "strong" (although they might not have been characterized as such at first blush) eliminate the "weak" without any qualms.

Of course, three objections can be made to the Darwinian vision of the evolution of the living. First, other approaches to evolution, those closer to our sense of compassion, are possible; second, Darwinian evolution pertains to our *past*, but there is no reason it must continue in the *future*; and finally, following the philosopher David Hume, we cannot derive normative prescriptions from states of affairs in the world.

Theorists of evolution such as Peter Kropotkin very presciently have attempted to demonstrate that principles of cooperation and mutual assistance are just as fundamental as the more typically cited phenomena of competition and selection. More recent specialists in animal behavior, such as the primatologist Frans de Waal, take the same tack but show that the evolution of living beings is only partly cooperative, which is something altogether different. The principles of cooperation at work in evolution tend to be combined with the original Darwinian principle of cruelty, which they are far from replacing. The world is not completely black and white but a mixture of both. We have known this since the beginning of time, but, curiously, we have to remind ourselves of it constantly.

As for the belief that Darwinism pertains to our past and has no relevance to our present, it is an appealing yet false illusion, as Lewis Carroll demonstrates elegantly in *Alice in Wonderland* through the character of the Red Queen. She explains to Alice that Alice must keep running in order to stay in the same place. From an evolutionary perspective, every living being needs to keep transforming itself even if it has reached a state that is satisfactory for it. Unless a species can stop evolution itself, which is a priori beyond the reach of a normal living being, it is tasked with transforming itself *ad vitam aeternam*. In this sense, there will always be cruelty in the world; to deny cruelty is to deny the world and thus to disappear pure and simple.

Finally, Hume's principle (to which frequent references are made by those who have done a little philosophy and want to disconnect ethical action from material contingencies in this lowly world) has in general been poorly interpreted. A pragmatic empiricist, Hume would not have supported the idea that we need not take the world into account in order to act morally. He refused to consider empirical reality to be the *sole* criterion for norms that are to be followed, but he certainly did not advocate treating the test of reality as irrelevant to the determination of ethical stances. And even vegetarians do not refrain from appealing to empirical research when they justify their position—for example, when they demonstrate that animals really suffer. I do not mean to suggest that nature forces us to kill but rather that predation has occupied a central place in the world as long as carnivores have existed and that it is only with difficulty that we can consider an everyday condition of so many living beings to be a perversion unless we assume that human beings can be moral *against* nature. In other words, wanting to establish ethical norms *on the basis of* nature and supposing that it is ethical to behave *against* nature have more than a little in common with one another. In both cases, the moral claim arises on the basis of a pointedly uncritical relationship to the dynamic of nature. I can understand that a vegetarian is averse to killing a living being, but this does not mean that an ethical transgression is involved in the killing.

Acting legitimately does not always mean acting in a gentle manner, and not all violence is intrinsically illegitimate. It is not normal for a child to act violently, but forbidding a child to have any recourse to violence or insulating a child from violence altogether will prevent the child from developing properly and becoming a balanced and creative human being. A life without violence toward another animal might be more ethical (and, again, this is open to question), but it would be lacking something essential compared with a life that is truly worth living. Thus, we should be suspicious of vague analogies with situations in which consent is involved because these situations are in fact quite different from the ones we are considering.

Radically Remodeling Nature

From the foregoing we have to conclude that the ethical vegetarian is a person who *hates* nature *as it is* and who prefers nature *as he or she imagines it*.

The disgust that the vegetarian expresses toward the carnivore is fundamentally a disgust for animals—disgust that he conceals under concern for others and probably for himself. What the vegetarian dislikes is not so much meat as human beings themselves and animals. A human being who did not inflict any suffering on animals would simply no longer be a human being or even an animal, for a fundamental principle of animality is precisely suffering and causing to suffer, disturbing and being disturbed, harming and being harmed. Here again we must be clear: I am not saying that animals want to cause suffering or that they enjoy their own suffering but rather that suffering is an intrinsic part of an animal's nature. One may not like animals, but one cannot say that one likes animals and at the same time deny what constitutes a fundamental characteristic of animals.

Thus, the vegetarian is not *closer* to nature as he repeats over and over again; he instead finds nature utterly intolerable and attempts to create as much distance from it as possible. Of course, he will deny this assertion, but simply because *he never fully accepts the terms of his position* and the logical consequences of what he proposes.

Strictly speaking, a consistent vegetarian (the "deep" vegetarian, in contrast with the mundane and "superficial" vegetarian[9]) would have to be a militant prepared to eat only genetically modified organisms that came neither from animals nor from plants. Or, more precisely, a *truly coherent vegetarian* would have to fight for humanity's departure from the animal kingdom and for our transformation (by means of biotechnologies and nanotechnologies) into a new organism capable of surviving exclusively from photosynthesis, without any predatory activity whatsoever. A rigorously committed vegetarian would be committed to changing human beings biologically so that they become *posthumans of the future*—and this is a program that would look quite different from the rather laughable one advocated by a number of contemporary theorists of the posthuman, who want *only* to improve on the current condition of human beings.

A truly consistent vegetarian would also be committed to using biotechnology to turn *all* carnivores into vegetarians and to transform all prey animals born in the future so that they would reproduce no more than would be sustainable in the ecosystems in which they lived because those ecosystems would henceforth be devoid of predators. As soon as humanity becomes technologically capable of completely eradicating carnivorous animals, it would become *morally* obligated to do so.

The vegetarian's hatred of animals is perverse in that he justifies it by appealing to his love of animals. The vegetarian is an abusive animal, just as one speaks of an abusive mother. The vegetarian's misguided love seeks the death or the castration of those whom he purports to love, with the aim of replacing them with stuffed animals that give no offense and are often rather insubstantial.

Accepting Life

Generally speaking, the vegetarian, like the humanist, adopts an attitude of unacceptable arrogance when she makes a moral judgment about how life ought to be and how other beings ought to behave, for in doing so she places herself above other beings.

This vegetarian is an omnivorous animal who considers the dietary regimen of her species to be immoral. Such a "demonization" of the natural is not without precedent. We have seen movements campaign against sexuality (even though it is a normal form of behavior) and in favor of the subservience of women to men (even though, from a biopsychological point of view, women are perfectly autonomous and stand in need of no symbiosis with a mate). One may think that it is preferable not to eat meat, and that is perfectly acceptable; but it is only with difficulty that one can turn this position into a major ethical choice. The regime of meat eating is part of what it means to be human today, whether one likes it or not: we have an enzyme for digesting elastin, a fiber of animal origin, and we need vitamin B, a molecule produced exclusively by animals.

Donna Haraway makes the same point when she notes that in denying a specific feature of the living the vegetarian's position is fundamentally a fatal ideology. As she argues, there is not nor has there ever been a living being that lives without exploiting *at least* one other living being.[10] In this respect, the vegetarian purports to want to protect living beings at all costs but is in fact opposed to them.

As the American poet Gary Snyder says facetiously, "Everything that breathes is hungry"![11] Eating—that is, eating other living beings—is part of animal life, and the desire to change life reflects unacceptable vanity. Buddhism, whose adherents include Gary Snyder, is aware of the impossibility of eradicating all suffering, and it has never issued the demand that suffering be eliminated; it satisfies itself with the endeavor to reduce suffering within the limits of what is possible and reasonable for us to do, and it is especially concerned with eliminating *needless* suffering.

For the feminist Sharon Welch, we are not capable of changing in a unilateral way. The ethics of control, which seeks to reach its objective without taking others into account, needs to be replaced by an ethic of risk, which accepts the fact that our ability to change ourselves and the world is limited but also requires us to take full responsibility for our actions.

Vegetarians systematically overlook the fact that eating meat has a fundamental significance and that it teaches us a lesson about humility in that it reminds us of the interdependence of all living beings. Of course, the vegetarian might respond that she derives her existence from the plants she consumes, but, strangely, there are no vegetarians today who claim to be making themselves one with plants! The vegetarian instrumentalizes plants by denying them any real participation in life and by taking the same attitude toward plants that she reproaches the carnivore for taking toward animals. The vegetarian's choice is always a negative one: she does not choose vegetables but rather refuses meat.

I would next like to outline a carnivorous ethics, one that expresses an attitude that is not only rather humble and realistic but also more courageous than it might at first appear.

SECOND COURSE

The Ethics
of the Carnivore

ANY DEMONSTRATION OF THE TIMIDITY, the contradictions, and the paradoxes of vegetarian rhetoric needs to be accompanied by a positive account of the carnivore's outlook if we are to defend its legitimacy. We should grant to the vegetarian that the justifications typically offered for meat eating are themselves rather inconsistent. They invoke a weak form of utilitarianism and fail to provide serious responses to genuine questions posed by the vegetarian. One sees this in connection with the dietary aspect of the situation—the need for protein, for example. On this question, the weight of scientific evidence has reached its limit today; it would not be difficult to devise healthful artificial proteins to replace the animal proteins we need, and we could certainly satisfy ourselves with vegetable protein. In general, carnivores have trouble defending their conduct. All too often, they manifest a shameful and defensive attitude that is neither convincing nor effective as a response to the aggression of the vegetarian with whom they find themselves in conflict.

A defense of meat eating is, however, possible on purely ethical grounds. The fundamental rules of life apply to all human beings without exception, and one of the most important principles for preserving harmony on earth is precisely the one that vegetarians reject most vigorously: the principle of reciprocity and exchange between living beings. A special consequence of this principle is an infinite debt on humanity's part to other animals and the ethical obligation to commemorate this debt constantly.[1] Thus, a human being cannot become an ethical vegetarian but rather must be an ethical carnivore. To see the contrast as being between the ethical vegetarian and the boorish carnivore would be too simple.

A Portrait of the Carnivore as a Predator

Among the mammals shaped by fifty-four million years of evolution, 237 carnivorous species—from the pygmy weasel, which weighs forty-five grams, to the brown bear at fifteen hundred pounds—are descended from a single ancestor. The carnivores comprise eight families: canids, martens, bears, racoons, genets and civets, mongooses, hyenas, and felines. In fact, only 36 percent of carnivores have a dietary regimen composed of more than 60 percent prey. But it should be noted that more than half of the large predators (those that weigh more than forty-five pounds) eat only meat.

Humans, like other apes, are not carnivores sensu stricto, even though we have many things in common with social groupings of gregarious carnivores and primates. Like chimpanzees, humans are omnivores. Thus, *Homo sapiens* should be characterized as a species that *also* eats meat. Human beings can eat meat, but they are not required to do so. Here it is the carnivorous dimension of the omnivore that interests me—in particular, the way in which this dimension has shaped humanity.

The philosopher Paul Shepard is acutely interested in this question. He explains that carnivores and herbivores, in contrast with omnivores, are specialists. What I eat conditions not only my relations with the animals I consume but also my relationship to the world generally. Thus, the controversy surrounding the carnivore cannot be reduced to a question of diet. Nor is it simply a matter of the ethics of compassion. Being an omnivore, which means being partly a carnivore, is a fundamental existential state of being whose subtleties must be understood before we seek to eliminate it by force. Being a carnivore, even partly, is tied up at the deepest level with what it means to be human. The question is not simply whether we can be human without being carnivores but whether we would have become humans without having been carnivores and what importance this heritage has for us today.

Making a Big Deal (or Simply a Meal) out of a Dead Animal

In a recent text entitled "Eating Meat and Eating People," the philosopher Cora Diamond asserts, a bit harshly, that all considerations of animals' right not to be killed in order to be eaten miss the point.[2] If it were really a matter of rights, nothing would prevent a vegetarian from eating a dead animal that had not been killed for the purpose of being eaten—for example, an animal that died after being hit by a car. Nor would anything prevent a vegetarian from eating a cow accidentally killed by lightning. We could go even further than Diamond and note that a practicing vegetarian who did not want to kill the animal he wanted to eat could invent electronic means for locating an animal that had just died from natural causes to make a meal of it.

Cannibalistic Thoughts

Diamond gets to the crux of the matter when she compares the arguments offered by vegetarians to arguments made against cannibalism. Simply put, a human being is not good to eat, and considerations of the suffering that would be caused by killing the person are entirely beside the point because that is not where the problem lies. For Diamond, we simply cannot understand what is ultimately at stake here if we do not acknowledge that there is an essential difference between human beings and animals. The vegetarian presents a weak justification inasmuch as she appeals exclusively to the capacities of the animals in question. For Diamond, it is not in virtue of any specific features of humans that we do not eat them but rather because not being eaten by another human is part of what it means to be human.

Diamond's argument is all the more interesting for being open to a *twofold* debate. A vegetarian could respond that we might be able to alter our conceptions of animals such that eating them would no longer be acceptable. And an extreme (but completely logical) carnivore might argue that Diamond's position would permit us to eat people; all we would need to do this would be to change our conception of what is human—not a lot, but just a little.

This idea might appear shocking at first blush because most people do not realize the extent to which cannibalism is already present in our culture. Indeed, ours is one of the most cannibalistic cultures ever to have existed, with the exception of the Mayans. A human cannibal[3] is typically defined as a human who eats his or her fellow creatures. But we are not dealing with mathematical logic here, and our definitions can be revised in accordance with the relevant point of view. In the case under consideration, we can characterize the cannibal as someone who metabolically assimilates the flesh of his fellow creatures. This characterization would lead to the conclusion that organ grafts are also instances of cannibalism. Here, however, it would be a matter of *nonnutritive cannibalism* (one metabolizes the other without eating the other) and of *consuming carrion* (one contents oneself with metabolizing what one can of the other when one finds him dead but does not kill him). In other words, we live in cultures that practice a sort of kitchenless cannibalism (in contrast with the cannibal practices described by anthropologists)—a cannibalism of the raw rather than of the cooked.

The Ecology of Metabolic Assimilation

The xenografts discussed earlier shed unexpected but exciting light on the question of metabolic assimilation, which ultimately signifies *eating*. In fact, one can ask whether someone who has received a pig kidney is still an authentic human. From a strictly biological point of view, that individual will be a species of human–porcine hybrid—the frontier has not been crossed, but it has been rendered porous. Even more interesting, this grafted human is constituted (or, rather, reconstituted) through the assimilation of a pig part. Here we lack an ecology of organs—that is, of laws that would permit us to know what each organ becomes in a body, which relations it maintains with other organs apart from the functionalities proper to it, and which representations (symbolic or otherwise) we have of it that enable us to accept it as our own. In the same way, we stand in need of an ecology of the metabolic assimilation of the other. In this connection, the vegetarian's objections take on an entirely different significance. Indeed, the vegetarian appears as one who refuses to metabolize the animal, to make the animal enter into herself. The vegetarian does not want to *expose herself to the animal*—and the question is exactly what this signifies.

Eating Justly

The case of the Algonquin of Canada provides an especially rich avenue for thinking about this question. For them, according to descriptions provided by Marie-Pierre Bousquet, the problem is not one of killing the animal but rather of knowing *how* to kill it, *why* one is killing it, and what one then does with its corpse. Killing an animal to feed oneself is acceptable, provided that the means of killing entails the least possible suffering for the animal. The Algonquin add that it is necessary to be involved in a process of reciprocity and debt with regard to the animal so as to maximize the products yielded by the body. This last point is fundamental: the animal can be eaten in a just manner only if everything edible in the animal is actually consumed and everything usable is used. What matters is not killing an animal but rather doing so without needless suffering and not wasting anything of the one we have killed. *A contrario*, killing an animal for entertainment or to get rid of it is unacceptable in the eyes of the Algonquin.

At the topmost level, the carnivore's point of view can be considered in terms of the Algonquins' perspective on hunting and the consumption of meat. In their societies, both sorts of activity take place in a system of reciprocal giving—that is, in a somewhat sophisticated system of dependence. The fact of killing an animal in order to eat it leads the hunter to become involved with others of her kind. The animal can be killed and eaten only by respecting a highly restrictive commitment. The Algonquin does not instrumentalize the animal, and she admits that a fundamental characteristic of life consists in a form of cruelty that it is neither possible nor desirable to eliminate. Thus, the Algonquin's attitude is the opposite of that of the vegetarian, who instrumentalizes vegetation and adopts a "Disneyesque" vision of the world in refusing to grant (and to accept) the least place for cruelty in the space of the living.

A vegetarian might object here, and rightly so, that the Algonquin live in an ecosystem (the great forests of Canada) rich in meat and poor in edible vegetation and that for them eating meat is a nutritional choice essential to survival. There is some basis for this remark, but it is not especially pertinent to the question that occupies us here. That the Algonquin have to engage in predation to feed themselves does not necessarily mean that the provision of protein constitutes the heart of the phenomenon, even though it is seen in these terms both by carnivores who perceive in meat nothing more than a substance containing protein and by vegetarians who conceive of predation exclusively in terms of aggression. For their own part, the Algonquin have developed an *ethically positive* approach to meat, and the temptation of vegetarianism does not make a lot of sense to them. Indeed, the mere fact that I am obligated to choose a particular option in a given situation does not mean that this option is necessarily negative for me.[4]

An Ethic of Dependence

The Algonquin example shows that the carnivore's ethics initially takes the form of an ethic of reciprocity that can be extended further. Thus, one may consider that energies must circulate in the world and that it is the good circulation of these energies that establishes both harmony and justice. Each is the condition for the existence of the other, and predation in general constitutes one of the principles of this harmony.

This ethic of reciprocity involves significant restrictions, for it is an ethic of dependence with which we find ourselves confronted. This point is important because it is precisely the notion of predation that shocks the vegetarian. For the vegetarian, predation is above all aggression inflicted by one living being on another, and it must be reduced as far as possible, if not eliminated altogether. But such a negative view of predation is by no means the only one possible. One can conceive it in more positive terms as the fundamental form of dependence that grounds our relationship to animals. Assuming one's role as a predator, in other words, amounts to recognizing that one's existence depends on that of others—and that the existence of others can depend on one's own existence. All animals are predators, even herbivores such as cows, who feed on grass. It is equally true that plants, such as certain African acacias, alter the chemical composition of their leaves when they are attacked by antelopes, thereby becoming toxic to their attackers. This clearly shows that the acacias perceive the actions of herbivores to be acts of aggression. There is no need for me to be delighted by this, but it would be absurd for me to view it as a metaphysical scandal.

To Eat an Animal Is to Make Oneself Dependent

Thus, a fundamental theme in ethics is that of codependence: whoever eats an animal takes on a dependence with regard to it. To reduce the Algonquin's consumption of meat to a biological necessity is narrow and reductive. As Paul Shepard writes, in the first instance animals are ingested by human beings as a substance, and then they are ingested in a process of thought before ultimately being incorporated into our psychological structures.[5] Therefore, the question of predation should be considered in terms of its global significance and extended as far as possible. The human being's relation of dependence vis-à-vis the animal is not as special as that. All living beings are involved in forms of dependence with other living beings. Here there is a principle that is constitutive of life. There is a twofold advantage to being aware of this principle. It reminds us of everything we owe to others and sets a limit, particularly in a quantitative sense, to that which can be taken. To take more than what is necessary is ruled out: no act of predation may place the system in danger. Thus, eating comes back not only to taking on a dependence but also to accepting one's involvement in it. To eat an animal is to refuse to believe that human beings enjoy a state of exception in the sphere of animality. Assuming one's position as a carnivore, in other words, constitutes a posture of humility in comparison with the vegetarian, who purports to situate himself above the animality of which he is in fact a part. The vegetarian, as we saw in the first course of this discussion, can be characterized as a human being who refuses to let herself be intoxicated by other animals. Here we distance ourselves even further from the vegetarian vision of peaceful coexistence devoid of reciprocal contamination.

Two points must be emphasized. The first is that dependence here, far from being a passive posture, is on the contrary a very active posture. The second is the need to conceive the positive dimension of dependence in a culture that constantly insists on autonomy and for which such an attitude constitutes a real challenge. We think all too quickly that dependence is something negative. Nonetheless, the philosopher Gabriel Marcel, among others, strongly criticized the idea of autonomy. For him, a vigorous life requires exposing oneself to and accepting confrontation. To refuse to place oneself in danger or to suffer and to refuse to place others in danger and make them suffer are utterly antithetical to life.

Making Oneself Worthy to Receive

An important aspect of the philosophy of the hunter-gatherers is usually greatly minimized when one envisages the operations of reciprocity in terms of the giving and receiving of gifts, which is of special interest to Marcel Mauss. The capacity to receive is in fact at least as fundamental as the capacity to give; in the very process of living, what is at stake is just as much the existential gift of oneself and of others. No doubt it would be necessary to return to the Christian theology of grace in order to find such a perspective. The reading of Mauss undertaken by Jacques Derrida is, from this point of view, quite illuminating when he explains that the true gift is precisely that which cannot be repaid. The animal's gift of itself gives rise to the hunter's dependence not on the animal that has been eaten (it is not alive!) but on those who have not been eaten and on those who are responsible for them. For this relation is not established exclusively between animal and hunter but between the hunter, the hunted animal, and the spirit that protects it.

Thus, the ethical imperative is not simply not to take anything without giving something, but above all not to take anything without first having received and to accept this gift. Never be an egoistic predator *who refuses to receive*. When the Indians kill their prey, they thank its "spirit" for this "gift," and they do so in such a manner that the species itself continues to proliferate and its members are able to live in good conditions. The question of spirit is important, whatever its nature may be. What matters is that the dependence created by the fact of eating an animal is located on a plane of existence that is not under the hunter's control. One can always come to terms with an animal; it is much more difficult to come to terms with its "spirit." To see the hunter's obligation to the animal in terms of nothing more than enlightened self-interest is to have a deformed and false vision of what is at stake. One is involved not in a negotiation with interlocutors who are more or less cunning but rather in a fundamental alienation that is finally and paradoxically the forfeit of one's autonomy.

This point is essential because dependence thereby acquires a permanence that cannot easily be overcome. As a consequence, eating meat becomes a particularly strong form of addiction. But we are talking about a positive addiction, a constructive one, not a negative and destructive addiction.

The notion of addiction might appear to be out of place here because today addiction is systematically associated in a negative way with the consumption of drugs. But as Avital Ronell explains, so far no one has defined satisfactorily what counts as a drug, and any substance can a priori serve as one.[6] Thus, meat is perfectly amenable to playing this role.

An Existential Ethics

But in what sense is this situation of dependence pertinent for someone like me, who does not necessarily believe in spirits? Such a question, which is posed even by the vegetarian, can be discussed productively only if one is interested not in the nature of spirit but in its function. Dealing with "spirit," whatever it may be in other respects, returns us to a recognition of the fact that I can be fully human only by negotiating with what surpasses me. The skeptical vegetarian will insist once again, In what sense is it necessary to eat an animal? The response is simple: it is only in a process as fundamental as that of death or metabolic ingestion that I can place myself in such a situation of dependence. It is only in a transaction involving my existence and that of others that I can live and can permit others to live—"permit" meant here in the practical rather than the juridical sense.

Here I by no means place myself in an ethic of compassion (where I would care for the other because he or she suffers and where I would suffer from knowing that he or she suffers) nor in an ethic of equality (where I would care for the other because he or she is as intelligent as I), but rather in an ethic of shared life (I care for the other because the other is the condition for my existence and I the condition for the other's existence). In this context, the question of suffering is altogether secondary, not because it is legitimate to make an animal suffer (this is never the case), but because what is important certainly goes beyond suffering.

Two Major Mistakes: Greed and Pride

From the standpoint of this ethic of predation, two grave mistakes must be avoided at all costs. The first consists in wanting to escape this system, the second in abusing it. Escaping the system means not respecting its modalities, either by means of greed (in taking more than what is permitted) or by means of pride (in considering oneself a living being above the living, not subject to what connects living beings to one another without exception). Thus, on the one hand, the vegetarian commits the sin of pride in purporting to place herself outside the stakes of life. On the other hand, the hypercarnivore of contemporary Western societies commits the sin of greed in engaging in an excessive consumption of meat that does not correspond to any fundamental dependence.

The Language of Hunger

The defense of the carnivore that I propose here is fundamentally ethical. When vegetarians proclaim their refusal to eat meat, they posit "what is eaten" (the animal) from the very start as if it were prior to the metabolic processes involved in the bodily assimilation of the animal. What does the animal body of the human being become if he no longer eats meat? One will object here that vegetarian or frugivorous animals are not the problem. This is true, but vegetarians no longer consider themselves to have emerged from animality; indeed, Western beings cling to this belief in nonanimality with the diseased insistence of a pretentious little monkey. From this point of view, Darwinism establishes for many people not that they are animals but rather that they once were, which is a different matter altogether. We must eat meat because doing so reminds us constantly that we ourselves are animals born of the flesh of other animals and are in a position to feed other animals. Eating an animal, in other words, is a positive way of affirming our fundamental animality and our constitutive proximity to other animals. This metabolic connection establishes beyond question our continuity with the animal, first because we thereby affirm that our body is their body but also because we admit that we are taking part in what it means to be an animal and in particular what it means to be involved in the stakes of life and death that characterize animality.

Vegetarians Do Not Want to Become Closer to Plants, But Rather to Distance Themselves from Animals

At this point, the vegetarian will object that the situation is exactly the same for plants. By eating plants, we assert our fundamental contiguity with vegetables, grains, and fruits. This could be true, but it is never what vegetarians insist on; on the contrary, they always justify their regimen from the very start not by positing the need to *become closer* to plants but rather by positing the need to *distance themselves* from animals. But this is not a straightforward matter. Can we truly distance ourselves from animals? Ernst Bloch notes quite rightly that human beings have not only retained their animal drives but *also produced new ones*.[7] The animal dimension of human beings is not a remote remnant of the past but an intrinsic aspect that is constantly reactualized. *We constantly reactivate our animal past*; it is utterly illusory to believe that we can ever successfully get rid of it. The animal dimensions of the human being are not to be classified among the residues of a more or less obscure past; they are the essential constituents of the human. It is absurd to believe that one day there will exist a human being deprived of animality. Not only is it in the very nature of a human being to be animal, but *this animality can itself become transformed over time.*

Language Is Not a Substitute for the Predatory Relationship

A second, more subtle objection is that language allows us to think our proximity to the animal without having to eat the animal. Here language would play the role of a substitute for the predatory relationship. It would enable us to understand that we are animals. This objection is too intellectual to be taken seriously. It assumes from the start that language can be a convincing substitute for what the body experiences. It is a little like saying to someone that there is no need to have sexual relations, that it is enough to speak of sex, or that rather than feeding oneself, one may satisfy oneself with speaking of feeding oneself. More than anything else, to make this claim is to misunderstand altogether the significance of our metabolic connection with animals.

Living Our Convergence with Animals, Not Simply Dreaming It

The central pillar of my argument is that our relationship to animality cannot be purely conceptual; we must truly *live it*, metabolically, in our biological and behavioral body and not simply simulate it in an analytical fashion. This is exactly what is expressed by the philosophy of the Anishinabe of North America, a philosophy according to which the concept of hunting relates back to apprenticeship in the sense that such experiences are ways of connecting ourselves to other creatures possessing an existence. More than a simple search for prey, hunting corresponds to an attempt to understand the hunted animal and to renew and extend[8] the awareness we have of our intense proximity with other animals. Moreover, language is a capacity with two sides: it is capable of the worst as well as the best, as the Greeks quite precociously understood. Before being a capacity on which human beings pride themselves, it is also a handicap of which we must be highly suspicious, particularly when it enables us to adduce truncated reasoning that gives us the illusion that we have already departed from animality.

We Can Pet the Animal Rather Than Eat It
(But We Can Also Pet It and Eat It)

A third objection posed by the vegetarian rests on the idea that in order to establish intimate connections with animals we must *pet* them rather than *eat* them. Expressed in this concise manner, the objection might appear a little ridiculous, but for all that it is entirely pertinent. It is indeed possible to develop very satisfying relationships with an animal without eating it. However, this situation, which occurs for example with companion animals, is not easily generalizable and encounters real limits. Moreover, the question under discussion is not "How do we live in peace with a favorite companion animal?" I am attempting to elaborate a philosophy of identity rather than one of neighborly relations. What interests me is less a matter of knowing how to share one's life with a familiar animal than of knowing what it means for a human being to have to share his life with other animals. A quick reading will not make it possible to see the difference between the two; a deeper reading is needed to perceive a fundamental opposition. It is less a matter of being nice to animals than of making one's fundamental animality explicit and accepting it completely. In this way, one can pet an animal and eat it at the same time.

Devising New Ways to Eat Meat

The vegetarian's role is ultimately a positive one. After reading all of my criticisms of the vegetarian, the reader may be surprised by such a reversal and charge me with inconsistency, but this would be to misunderstand me. The vegetarian who refuses to eat any meat has gone astray. But she sends the carnivore an important message that the latter would do wrong not to heed. The truth is that eating meat is never a benign matter. This is what we are told by the Algonquin, whom I used as a guiding thread earlier in this chapter. The vegetarian concludes from this truth that we ought to give up the consumption of meat altogether. In coming to this conclusion, the vegetarian reduces the ingestion of meat to a simple dietary practice, even though it is more than that. Many vegetarians justify their refusal to eat meat by arguing that we must not kill animals or cause them to suffer. I have shown that the situation is considerably more complex than vegetarians suppose.

Some vegetarians say something else that is worth considering quite seriously. I call these people "political" vegetarians in contrast with the "ethical" vegetarians I have considered so far.[9] These political vegetarians suggest that the regular consumption of meat by a population that numbers in the billions is more than deadly; it is insane. This argument has to be taken seriously. Factory farming is a disgrace, and the carnivore can only agree with the political vegetarian's assessment. And when the latter observes that the current population can eat meat only if it is produced by means of factory farming and that the only way to end factory farming is to cease the consumption of meat, this reasoning merits at least some consideration. In rich countries, the consumption of meat has become a habit that no longer involves any hint of commemoration or communion. Thus, the political vegetarian's argument has nothing in common with the ethical vegetarian's; what the former is concerned with is a horrible truth that even a carnivore has to acknowledge. At the same time, we must remain sensitive to the limits of the vegetarian's position. One can perfectly well campaign for a drastic *reduction* in the consumption of meat without necessarily *forbidding* it, just as one can campaign for a reduction in the human birth rate. Moreover, vegetarians tend to overlook the specifically political dimension of food production. The Nobel Prize–winning economist Amartya Sen has shown that famines have been primarily political and ultimately have little to do with a country's available food supply.

A final point is always left out of the discussion, even though it merits careful consideration: caring for millions of carnivorous companion animals (dogs and cats) has extensive harmful consequences, and yet numerous vegetarians live with these companions. To what extent do vegetarians bear responsibility for them? Of course, one can always try to make one's dog a vegetarian, but, to employ a euphemism, doing so borders on animal abuse. Strictly speaking, a consistent vegetarian would not only refuse to have any companion animals but would campaign for their elimination—for example, by demanding the systematic sterilization of existing companion animals. Of course, this is an impossible task. But the choice does not become one of either having carnivorous companion animals or not having them. Substantially reducing the number of carnivorous companion animals is certainly a serious option; it would benefit fish, seed-eating birds, and omnivorous birds such as corvids and crows, all of which possess personalities at least as rich and complex as those of the carnivorous animals to which we give preferential treatment. But acknowledging this fact forces us to be open to discussion regarding the consumption of meat—not only by human beings but also by those carnivores who share life with us.

The dangers to the environment posed by meat eating are not imaginary, and they must be taken seriously; but is there, for all that, an aporia in the carnivore's position? It is a bit hasty to assume that there is. Between the trivialized consumption of anonymous meat and a completely vegetarian diet, there is in fact a third way that neither vegetarians nor carnivores in contemporary

Western countries have seriously explored: eating meat in a limited, ritual fashion. This means making each meal with meat into a ceremony or commemoration, consuming meat only on these occasions, and making sure that the only meat we consume in these situations comes from animals that were well treated.

Claude Lévi-Strauss wrote something in an article in *La Repubblica* on November 24, 1996, that I endorse wholeheartedly:

> Agronomists will attempt to increase the amount of protein in plants used for food, while chemists will attempt to produce synthetic proteins in industrial quantities . . . [but] the appetite for meat will never disappear. Opportunities for the satisfaction of this appetite will become rare, costly, and filled with risk. (Japan has experienced something similar with the *fugu* or blowfish, which is said to have an exquisite taste but which is deadly if not prepared correctly.) Meat will have a place on the menu in exceptional circumstances. One will consume it with the same mixture of pious reverence and anxiety that, according to ancient mariners, was observed at the cannibalistic meals of some societies. In both cases, it is a matter of having communion with one's ancestors as well as of being exposed to the risks and dangers posed by living beings that were or have become one's enemies.[10]

Thus, what is needed is to devise new ways to eat others and by the same token—it is the least we can do—to be eaten. For the real scandal is not eating animals but eating them too much and not wanting to be eaten by them. One ought to be able to offer up one's body to be eaten by animals. This idea will appear shocking to some, but we give our bodies to science, so why not to animals? Not all societies are equally hesitant about such practices. The Sioux, for example, leave their cadavers out in the open, exposed to animals. In Western countries, the hard line on this matter was tempered by faulty technologies. One of the great advantages of traditional coffins was that they could be buried in the ground, and worms and bacteria could dine at their leisure on the cadavers inside them. Cremation can be considered the theft of a cadaver (even if we can reuse the ashes), and cryogenic freezing can be considered a completely unethical practice because the people who insist on it refuse to let their bodies return to the great exchange among the living.

In a very classical fashion, the debate between carnivores and vegetarians has become exclusively about ethics or diet. Is it possible to develop new approaches to the dispute between carnivores and vegetarians? I can offer a hint about what I have in mind here. So far no attention has been paid to a major difference between eating meat and eating only plants, even though it opens up some interesting perspectives: a diet of meat leaves things behind—bones in particular—whereas a diet of plants leaves nothing behind. To this extent one might consider the vegetarian to be the one who does not want to leave any traces of his meal. Until now, art has expressed little creative interest in this question, and the notion of what remains might be profitably exploited. But this may be more an artistic endeavor than a philosophical agenda.

A SORT OF DESSERT

PARADOXICALLY, THIS BOOK IS WRITTEN more for vegetarians than for carnivores, even though it will do more to shock the former than the latter. One of the significant problems with which vegetarians are faced is that they are operating in a closed circuit and are not developing critical discourses about their practices and their fundamental standpoint. Here we encounter an ambiguity shared by every discourse that seeks to be both theoretical and militant. An analogy will shed some light on this ambiguity: there is no question that the evolution and fortification of Christianity, quite apart from what one may think about it in other respects, have been inspired much more by the work of critical thinkers than by that of hagiographers.

Most people who become vegetarians do so for reasons having nothing to do with morality. They refrain from eating meat either because they do not like it or because they believe that eating only plants, fruits, and cereals is better for their health. One hardly hears from these people because they do not have any demands to make. After all, nobody forbids an exclusively vegetarian diet in our culture. The ethical vegetarian's view, a minority one, has an entirely different status, even though (or rather because) the tenets of ethical vegetarianism are highly problematic. One of the aims of this text has been to take this position seriously by seeking to uncover its fundamental presuppositions (in particular the belief that there is a position of innocence and that an ethics of

83

life can be established on the basis of a fundamental opposition between animal and plant) and draw out its logical conclusions.

The fact is that a rigorous vegetarian position has implications that the majority of vegetarians are not prepared to accept, such as the need to transform human beings into plants and the need to eradicate every form of animality from the earth. Some ethical vegetarians (not all and perhaps not the majority) can certainly be considered religious fundamentalists who attach the greatest importance to their convictions and believe that they must spread their gospel throughout the world. Such vegetarians do not content themselves with eschewing the consumption of meat; they want the entire world to do as they do, and on some occasions they are prepared to employ force to make this happen. This militancy, which is often aggressive, seems to me to be characteristic of Western ethical vegetarianism.

The ethical vegetarian's position is far from innocuous. Friedrich Nietzsche was one of the first thinkers to exhibit a frank skepticism in the face of moral claims, and one of his most significant discoveries was the recognition that *every morality has its price*. There is no reason to consider ethical vegetarianism to be an exception.

Ethical vegetarianism constitutes an objection to animals themselves. Paradoxically, it is the vegetarian who resurrects the humanist opposition between human and animal at a time when that opposition is proving to be more outmoded than ever. One might object that ethical vegetarians love animals, and this is often the case, but it is not a compelling response to the charge that the vegetarian is a segregationist who would like to separate human beings rigorously from animals. After all, it is also the case that many religious fundamentalists love children, but they are utterly disgusted by the conception of sexuality implied by that love. The vegetarian loves an extremely idealized animal, an animal that ultimately is no longer much of an animal.

On the vegetarian's view, concern for animals usually plays a role comparable to that played by concern for children in efforts to counter pornography. The parallel made by vegetarian theorists between the rejection of meat and the rejection of pornography occurs so often that it has to be more than a mere accident. The vegetarian loves animals in the same way that the opponent of pornography loves children. In both cases, the problem is the same: animals and children are instrumentalized in the name of causes that do not ultimately concern them. Vegetarians, in other words, use animals as weapons in a war against life itself. They never admit that life is dirty, bloody, repugnant, malodorous, unjust, cruel, and so on even though it also possesses immeasurable richness and great beauty. The attitude of innocence adopted by the ethical vegetarian is without question his most revealing characteristic. Ethical vegetarians believe that they can keep their stomachs pure even while they acknowledge that they are living beings. This is an extremely dangerous illusion. Walt Disney did not write the history of living beings; he wrote pretty stories for children.

The debates surrounding the vegetarian position are often less than completely satisfying because the ethical vegetarian overwhelmingly employs a mode of argumentation that brings together a prohibition (against eating meat) and a defense (of animals). Today prohibition and defense are like the two teats of a contemporary left form of thinking that has largely been abandoned by the imagination and utopia—by what the German philosopher Ernst Bloch rightly called the "principle of hope."[1] It is certainly no accident if Hans Jonas's sad "principle of responsibility" has eclipsed Bloch's "principle of hope," against which Jonas's principle was directed.[2]

By the same token, the carnivore's position has a fundamental ethical dimension, although this dimension is continually passed over in silence. If I dare say that there is no need to pay attention to carnivores, it is not because they have any difficulty defending their steak. Believing that the carnivore's position is reducible to a need for protein but the vegetarian's consists in a refusal to inflict suffering on animals amounts to dangerous nonsense. There is always peril in deluding oneself about the ethical claims that one is in fact making and in minimizing their significance and their ultimate implications.

In contrast with the vegetarian, the carnivore acknowledges that she is a living being in the midst of other living beings. She permits herself to become intoxicated by these other beings; she recognizes that she is nothing without them and that she is made from them, just as they are made from her. In this sense, the carnivore's ethics is an ethics of acknowledged dependence; the carnivore is open to receiving what life gives her. The carnivore's ethics is an ethics of addiction to other animals.

But the carnivore's position, too, has significant limits—specifically those pertaining to excessive consumption of meat in rich countries, which has led to factory farming and the destruction of the environment. If the ethical vegetarian's position cannot be strictly maintained, that of the political vegetarian presents itself today as a vital necessity. Is the solution to become a political vegetarian who is occasionally and ritually a carnivore? One can at least attempt to go down this road.

POSTFACE

IN THIS POSTFACE, I WOULD LIKE to return to one of the most important points in my essay and focus the discussion on it: factory farming is a scandal that constitutes a veritable crime against the living, and as such it must be stopped completely; but in the face of this enormous moral exigency, the posture of the ethical vegetarian (I will simply say "vegetarian" here) is theoretically problematic and counterproductive. In this connection, vegetarians make two major strategic errors. First, they seek to solve the problem by undertaking a useless boycott against meat and by issuing counterproductive invectives against meat eaters. Second, they think that the problem of meat factories is purely moral when in fact it is in large part political. Thus, they are convinced that they can solve the problem within the context of contemporary societies (in broad strokes, within socioliberal, materialist, atheistic democracies—"atheological societies") when in fact these societies are themselves part of the problem. The strategy of inspiring compassion and fundamentally criminalizing the carnivore has failed; we need to pursue more radical measures.

A Societal Revolution and a Radical Politics

Meat factories are the disquieting symptom of the extreme pathological residues left by the Enlightenment dream characteristic of contemporary liberal Western democracies. These residues find expression in a variety of criminal activities perpetrated on animals as well as in a troubling unresponsiveness to the widespread poisoning of our ecosystems. Thus, the problem of factory farming needs to be understood within the larger context of an overall war waged against the living, a war for which contemporary ecological disasters provide ample evidence and the consequence of which can only be collective suicide. The Enlightenment dream had a luminous face that held the promise of universal emancipation. It was on this promise that the theorists of enlightenment always focused. But this dream of peace and emancipation concealed a darker face that even the most reactionary critics of enlightenment did not want to see. This dream became transformed into a nightmare, and social democracies struggled to make themselves look "normal," something that they have not been for a long time now. Defenders of these democracies have always succeeded in making people believe that we are living in a dual system in which totalitarianism is the only possible alternative to social democracy. It hardly need be pointed out that these totalitarian states—fascist regimes that sully their image with violence and frustration as well as Communist regimes based on a massive misappropriation of hope—are even worse, but today it is not these states that possess the real power. Thus, it is misguided to want to deal with the problem of industrial meat without dealing with that of our societies' permanent suicidal aggression toward the totality of living beings on the planet. In the end, it is all the same problem. But this cannot be taken for granted. The best argument in favor of a more global perspective on the problem is that in spite of some individuals' laudable efforts, we have not managed to stop factory farming; on the contrary, the situation has worsened dramatically over the past twenty years, and there is no indication that it will come to an end someday. Thus, where the majority of vegetarians advocate reforms within Western liberal democracies, I advocate exploring new forms of political organization. So in this text I propose moving beyond Western liberal democracies toward *nonreligious, constitutional theocracies*; here I am thinking along the lines of constitutional monarchy or, to put it more precisely, *nonreligious, federal anarchotheocracies*. I am not saying that this is the solution to the problem of factory farming but rather that if we are to solve the problem, we need to be more daring than we have been up to now and test a hypothesis that has never been considered. But before discussing what might appear to be a mere provocation, let us examine more closely the reasons why such a drastic measure is called for. The fact is that the situation is not a desperate one; it has already moved beyond that point.

The Limitations of Human Intelligence as the Central Political Problem of the Twenty-First Century

One of the central political problems of the twenty-first century finds surprisingly little discussion in contemporary political theory, and that is the problem of the fundamental limitations of human intelligence.[1] The increasing technological complexity of the world has made it increasingly difficult to understand. From an evolutionary perspective one would say that human intelligence, originally theorized in terms of its adaptation to a given environment (namely, the Pleistocene), has fashioned an environment to which it is no longer adapted and in the face of which it is out of place and helpless. Günther Anders is the first to have formulated this hypothesis consistently by placing the limitations of human intelligence at the heart of his reflection on modern technology.[2] For him, the products of technology exceed our capacities for representation, and our responsibility for these products is all the more diminished. Moreover, we have learned to believe only what we are allowed to believe. Anders describes this with the somewhat shocking expression "blindness in the face of apocalypse." This blindness is the product of a double asynchronicity—that between human faculties in relation to one another and that between human beings and the things they produce. It is what Anders calls the "Promethean gap."[3] Thus, our instruments increasingly become decisions made in advance, decisions that have already been decided upon, even before we possess the very potential to decide.[4] The "bureaucracy of interdependent instruments" has become increasingly present, increasingly important, and increasingly complicated. Room for our freedom is shrinking all the more. The result is a world that is incomprehensible. As Anders writes, "It is not completely impossible that *we*, who make these products, are at the point of creating a world whose pace exceeds our capacity to keep up and which absolutely outstrips our capacity to 'understand,' a world that utterly exceeds our capacity for understanding, our imagination and our emotions, not to mention our responsibility."[5] Human beings are no longer equal to the things we produce, and this situation is all the more troubling as we make desperate efforts to be their equal. Here the German philosopher presents a modernized version of the nightmare of the sorcerer's apprentice. Anders's thesis is all the more forceful when it is applied to professional philosophers. On his view, specialists in critical thought are ultimately nothing more than faithful servants of the powers of the moment, nor have they ever been anything more than that because all they do is prudently focus their attention on whatever is "philosophically presentable," and all that remains is for its history to be written. In this connection, Anders makes reference to the atomic bomb (which has been of surprisingly little interest to philosophers), although his analysis can very effectively be applied to contemporary meat factories. He gives an indication of this application when he emphasizes that "the human is what he eats, and mass-humans are produced by making them consume mass products."[6] His analysis of the atomic bomb can be applied to meat factories without any significant changes: people "know" only in a superficial way, without knowing what they know, and they conduct their analyses through recourse to inadequate categories. Just as they did in connection with the atomic bomb, they think of meat factories only as "means," without realizing that the pair means–end no longer has any meaning today and that "the production of means has become the end of our existence."[7] Anders offers as evidence a number of means detached from the efforts required to obtain them as well as from the alienation that results from this detachment—fruits obtained without labor combined with labor that bears no fruit, labor that no longer has any meaning inasmuch as it produces incomprehensible fruits diluted by opaque forms of organization. As in the case of the bomb, the responsibility for meat factories cannot be attributed to anyone—and if no one is culpable, then we are all virtual accomplices. Anders is well aware that his approach is extreme, but he justifies it by exaggerating the situation. How are we to grasp the unbelievable as long as we remain within the reasonable? As he clearly states, it is not a question of knowing how humanity ought to go on existing but rather whether it ought to continue to exist inasmuch as humans are no longer the representatives of a new historical generation but instead members of a new species.

Introducing "Disembodied Minds" Into Politics

In accordance with Anders's proposal, let us engage in an extreme form of thinking and exaggerate the case of meat factories. Here it is important to note that we have to change our political regime if we are to eradicate factory farming. We must alter profoundly what it means to engage in politics. The time of reforms has failed, and we need to become more radical. Doing so requires a rupture in our habitual ways of thinking. To conceptualize the forms that politics can take in the future, we need to mobilize an excessive kind of thinking—we need to adopt a posture that is a priori extravagant and put its plausibility to the test. Thus, it is utterly extravagant today to open our thinking to "disembodied minds" (spirits, phantoms, ghosts, and so on) and to propose that a theocracy might ultimately be the only political regime capable of ending the scandal of industrial meat. When more reasonable perspectives prove to be sterile, intellectual risk taking becomes an asset. Welcome to the club for explorers of a nonstandard future.[8]

Now, how plausible can we make the hypothesis that the time has come to restore "disembodied minds" to politics as a way to help human beings ameliorate their sad lot? If Günther Anders is right and human intelligence has been outstripped by its own accomplishments, then we must possess sufficient intelligence to recognize the limitations of our intelligence and see that our salvation comes from somewhere else. But from where? The space of possibilities is not very large. It may be machines, or it may be the gods. But the scandal of meat factories may lead one to entertain doubts about the sensitivity of machines—I do not say this to offend them—and their desire to close these factories. There remains recourse to the gods or to their successors, "disembodied minds." This expression rings a bit strange in the ears of Westerners. More than three centuries of militant and intransigent materialism have left their traces in our auditory canals; even a five-year-old child can understand the expression, as Marx (Groucho, not Karl) might say. A central pillar of contemporary political philosophy is the conviction that politics plays itself out exclusively among human beings in the coordination of conflicting interests bearing on the sharing of material wealth and the domestication of those who may want a bit more of the pie than what the gluttons are ready to cede to them. This is a major mistake. Ecophilosophers such as Arne Naess have been challenging this fundamental dogma ever since the 1960s. For them, it is important to open politics to nonhuman natural beings such as animals, vegetables, fungi, and ecosystems themselves.[9] The success of this approach can be seen, among other things, in the fact that philosophers of the most generalist bent, such as Peter Sloterdijk, continue to take up this thesis in broader contexts.[10] And yet the boldness of these thinkers has fallen short of what it might be. We must dare to bring *all* nonhumans into politics, in particular those entities whose status is ambiguous; Westerners are alone in challenging the existence of these entities and in refusing to accept what everyone else accepts. Rejection is always expressed in the language of a bellicose rationality that is very puritanical and excessively intolerant. In all other cultures without exception (including technologically highly advanced cultures such as the Japanese), "disembodied minds" (namely, entities that are immaterial but capable of interacting with the most minute features of our ecosystems) are part of the everyday comedy of life and not simply for those people one too quickly characterizes as "credulous"—a term that is really meaningless inasmuch as endeavoring not to believe is still believing.

The main argument offered by the confirmed materialist has always been that those who invoke these "disembodied minds" are charlatans who deliberately seek to deceive others and, moreover, that the material progress that has substantially and dramatically improved the world affords the best argument in favor of a strictly materialist conception of the world. Such an attitude may still have found a receptive audience up to the middle of the twentieth century, even though the majority of the population was composed of impoverished peasants who sought greater comfort at any price; but nobody holds this view anymore, for at least three reasons. (1) This sectarian and positivist rationalism has thrust the world into an unprecedented ecological catastrophe that has led to a profound deterioration of our climate, the collapse of entire living ecosystems, and the poisoning of humanity on a large scale—the evidence of which includes an otherwise inexplicable proliferation of autoimmune diseases and cancers of all kinds. The ambitious claims made on behalf of materialism are no longer persuasive; and even though some religions have certainly gone to extremes, the pretext of a protest against them looks ridiculous in the face of the challenges with which human beings are faced in the twenty-first century. Pascal was more apposite when he wrote that "the heart has reasons that reason does not know." (2) The results of work in contemporary physics, such as the theory of the multiverse,[11] are difficult to grasp, but they reduce considerably (to put it mildly) the force of the kind of primitive materialism to which the most militant of materialists subscribe. (3) Fieldwork in anthropology demonstrates unambiguously that the question of "disembodied minds" is not easily reduced to a purely political game of deception and manipulation of others.[12] Whoever has any serious interest in healers, shamans, and other spiritual mediums will not be so easily dispossessed of a vision of the world that accords genuine significance to "disembodied minds"—unless it is by dint of particularly underhanded forms of intellectual dishonesty and a rejection on empirical grounds of the phenomena that we encounter.[13] To say that such minds exist, however, is by no means to prejudge the ontological status that one might attribute to them. To acknowledge that they can play a role and have a place in politics is not to imply that we know what they are, nor is it to imply that we might one day be able to know this and even less that such knowledge would ultimately have the least significance. In the end, we must recognize that politics is not simply a space for negotiation with partners who are visible but just as much a game with partners who are less visible in that one does not even know in a given situation whether they are actually involved in the game or not. In a time of great tragedy, the genuine rationalist is not one who rejects "disembodied minds" as sheer phantasms or a deception designed to manipulate naive souls but rather one who is prepared to consider *every* possibility that might render intelligible the *full* range of phenomena that at least some people encounter. This approach is at once empirical and completely nondogmatic, and contemporary transhumanists such as Nick Bostrom of Oxford University's Institute for the Future of Humanity make use of it.

Raymond Ruyer's Societies of the Long-Living

Now, philosophy has not been as silent on this subject as one might think. Raymond Ruyer (1902–1987), for example, was aware of the importance of making a place for "disembodied minds" in politics; he discussed what he himself called "societies for long life," and he developed a very original technological neo-Gnosticism in an effort to lend a certain force to this idea.

In a brilliant if somewhat odd essay, *Les cent prochains siècles: Le destin historique de l'homme selon la Nouvelle Gnose américaine* (The next hundred centuries: The destiny of the human according to the New American Gnosis),[14] he argues that future societies will of necessity be organized around a relationship to "disembodied minds" (or what he calls "great beings") inasmuch as other forms of society (broadly speaking, materialist-hedonist societies that are dominant today and can be characterized as either societies of drug addicts or societies of engineers) will simply have disappeared. His argument relies on a heuristic opposition that he sets up between "conquerors of space" and "conquerors of time." For him, the societies that will survive over the coming hundred centuries (the societies of the long-living) will be those that conquer time; the Jews constitute the paradigm case of such societies. Conquerors of time comprise those societies that are destined to survive because they are oriented on a simple imperative—to endure. These societies put into effect "responsive arrangements" that are designed to master time and are organized around beliefs, myths, and rites.[15] Ruyer writes, "The vitality of a people is not based on justice, equality, liberty, liberation, scientific truth, or the progress of great ideas, but rather on rootedness, myths, sustaining visions and ideas, everyday religion, fundamental paganism, and a heroic subconscious." Such societies accord a central place to communication and commerce with "the other Great Beings of the cosmos, with other consciousnesses, and with the Great Consciousness." Thus, those who will have a central role to play will be those whom Ruyer calls "scientific shamans":

For it is certain that suprahuman and supraindividual Great Beings, be they specific or nonspecific, exist; and the universe is a society of spirits capable of reason and meaning, having its ground in a space–time Subject, located inside—or outside—observable space, and exercising axiological gravitation—i.e., possessing the potential for values and meaning.... Those with spiritual power will be listeners, scientific shamans, prophets of a new Divinity who challenge the mass media in the process of disseminating their communications with the Suprahuman; in new religious wars, or in struggles over priesthood and empire, they will often seek to dominate temporal authorities rather than be subject to their control.

Religions of the future will be organized around "reverence for spiritual or 'psychist' guides"; approaches to the Gnosis of personal immortality will play a central role, and women will hold the power as "guardians of spiritual-Gnostic power." Ruyer is more inspired by a form of spiritualism than by contemporary religions of the Book. "The new system will be capable of faith in reincarnation, the transformation of the soul of the deceased into a protector-spirit, personal communication with the living, and sacred communication with suprahuman Great Beings, the directors of life in common, as in the doctrine espoused by Allan Kardec." He concludes: "Scientific Gnosis does not invent myths in order to see the face of God in them. It turns the world of science inside out, and the formless Mask takes on shape in conformity with the invisible Face." This notion of "turning the world inside out," which is central to the French philosopher's Gnostic vision, is explained in detail in his unexpected best seller *La Gnose de Princeton* (The Gnosis of Princeton), which he published with Fayard in 1974. For Ruyer, the human being is a psychic predator—an animal that feeds not only on *biological food* but just as much on *psychic food* (a fortifying and violent sight for voyeurs) and *spiritual food*, as Ruyer describes elsewhere.[16] Any political regime that neglects this dimension is destined for impotence the moment it has to make an essential and potentially unpopular decision.

Toward a Constitutional, Nonreligious Theocracy

Ruyer's approach, whatever difficulties it may have, has something in common with the approach taken by those who seek to close meat factories: it is capable of introducing a principle of authority that would run counter to the popular will (while ultimately being favorable to it) without capitulating to any kind of simplistic totalitarianism that would create problems rather than solve them. Ruyer invokes the "myth" of "Great Beings" but remains quite vague about the precise status of these beings. Nonetheless, since the 1970s he has restored a certain relevance to what I have called "disembodied minds." Might such minds play an auxiliary role in the endeavor to conceive a political space that would facilitate progress in the effort to close meat factories? Taking such "minds" seriously, at least as a working hypothesis, might ultimately help us to change our ways of thinking—and such a hypothesis is worth working out even if the pitfall of a deus ex machina must be avoided at all costs. But as the Austrian philosopher Paul Feyerabend said, all available resources must be mobilized; we are bound to make use only of those that offer real utility, and we are not intelligent enough to distinguish the good from the bad—he himself subscribed to an anarchist epistemology that could only raise the hackles of those who prefer their serious careers to the joys of unbridled creativity.[17] When the most reasonable solutions have clearly failed, there remain only less-orthodox solutions. As is often the case, a deeper truth is concealed by a seemingly obvious one. In this connection, establishing a "theocracy" that extends real hospitality to "disembodied minds" in politics is certainly a gamble, but it might well have a very high payoff. Let us see, then, how one might *rationally* bring such a gamble to fruition.

The intended benefit of the kind of theocracy I have been describing here would be to provide a cultural, social, and political context with sufficient incentive to close the meat factories—that is, sufficiently *coercive* to accomplish this and sufficiently *persuasive* to be acceptable to those who benefit more or less from such factories. The price to be paid for this theocracy is twofold: the introduction of "disembodied minds" into a Western political arena that has believed since the eighteenth century that it is a victory to have eliminated any spiritual dimension from the exercise of power and the granting of a power that is not easily controlled to those who are the intermediaries between these minds and human beings. The convergence of particular interests with the powerful institutionalization of commercial interests keeps things from changing, but this convergence would dissolve in the face of an even more powerful institutionalization that would bring about change. To reopen this accursed question of theocracies now becomes a calculated risk. Thus, we must naturally take certain basic precautions. It is not a matter of giving carte blanche to religious individuals with whom it is always disquieting to consider doing business—even when one employs the kind of tools that would be useful in dealing with them. This is why there is no reason the kind of theocracy that I have in mind here should be based on any sort of religion, and it is in the separation of religion and theocracy that, among other things, the possible success of such a political regime is to be found. This theocracy needs to be characterized as a mode of constitutional government that of necessity includes shamans,[18] who systematically communicate the views of the "disembodied minds" with whom they engage in an exchange about[19] the problems at hand and whose views they make public.[20] These shamans have the decisive advantage of not belonging to any constituted clergy. Their mode of conduct is very different. This theocracy will have to be *constitutional* (which is to say that it will operate according to a democratic model like that found in constitutional monarchies) or federal—with a mode of operation fairly close to the way the Iroquois Nations functioned in North America before the barbarism of the English and the French destroyed one of the greatest examples of democracy in history.[21] These democracies had a distinctive feature that interests me a great deal: they gave a role to the shaman who could communicate with "disembodied minds."

This last point leads us to the heart of the problem—namely, the status of these shamans who serve as spiritual intermediaries. The primary appeal of shamanism in the present context is that it has always been hostile to violence perpetrated specifically against nature and animals; Amerindian cultures are especially clear on this point.[22] The contemporary rise of Islam demonstrates that many peoples continue to have a need for spiritual teachings. The problem with Islamism is not the spiritual tension that undergirds it (and that is also found outside of Islam) but rather its anger, which is fueled by resentment, and its pointless desire for revenge. Thus, the unification of various shamans into a federal organization constitutes a politically interesting alternative to established religions.[23] Such a shamanic theocracy might become problematic if it left room for charlatans to pursue their own greatest happiness, but it is precisely in disorganized spaces that charlatans are able to prosper, not in an institutionalized space with strict rules.[24]

Three Objections

In this connection, one of the most problematic beliefs held by vegetarians may be that human beings can escape the trap of meat factories *simply* by reforming the liberal democracies in which they live. Two mutually incompatible interpretations of my proposition about constitutional theocracy are possible. The first, which is rationalist in the extreme, assumes that a situation as irrational as that of industrial meat can be resolved only by strategies that are themselves irrational and seek to mobilize "disembodied minds," which are certainly imaginary but psychologically very persuasive. On the second interpretation, institutions such as meat factories show that human beings have entered into a situation of complete cognitive bankruptcy in which what is *truly* needed is the urgent intervention of intermediaries from outside (whatever "outside" might mean here), a sort of relative guardianship that is certainly not without its dangers but is less dangerous than continuing on a path of self-destruction and making the world unlivable. Each of these interpretations has some degree of legitimacy. We need to work out new political models with a principle of authority (but not an authoritarian model) that allows for a revolution in our relationship with the living—and what I am calling *nonreligious constitutional theocracy*, a term that will ring a little strange in Western ears, is one such model. In the debacle in which the world is enmired today, every kind of help is welcome, and all alternatives are worth considering, even if they appear extravagant; after all, our contemporary democracies were utterly implausible in the Middle Ages, even for the most enlightened minds. The idea of replacing capitalist democratic regimes with nonreligious theocracies may be surprising in the cultural context of the West at the beginning of the twenty-first century; and although I write that such an idea is surprising, I would do better to say that it is downright shocking—but this reaction is certainly not sufficient grounds to reject the idea without further ado. Three objections to it come immediately to mind, all of which have straightforward responses: theocracies are always deplorable political regimes; "disembodied minds" do not exist; and it is not rational to be committed to the goals espoused by such minds.

1. The desire to establish a theocracy today may reasonably surprise more than one reader. We consider theocracies—that is, political regimes involving commerce with a god or gods—to be the most oppressive regimes in existence, regimes delivered over to the caprice of the clergy and leaving no room for opposition by a popular will. Thus, we associate caprice, abuse, and oppression with such political regimes. How can anyone want to return to an "obscurantist" political regime when we have lived through the French Revolution (which was just as antireligious as it was antiroyalist) and the joys of democratic systems that are more or less atheistic? The reality is clearly much more complex.[25] In the first place, the theocracy that I propose is not religious inasmuch as it gives a place to shamans but not to priests. The difference here, and it is an essential one, is that there is no homogeneous spiritual body in shamanism or a clergy that can exercise a monopoly on interpretation. Second, to the extent that such theocracies have respect for constitutions, they have no reason to be any more "obscurantist" than Western liberal democracies, which just happen to suffer from some major problems, the primary one being that they are incapable of facing up to the challenges that destabilize them and the rest of the world. If we do not content ourselves with mere words, and if we try to evaluate the situation objectively, without answering the question before we have even

posed it, it has got to be clear that Western democratic political regimes are on the verge of disaster. Not only have these democratic regimes failed to improve the lot of billions of people—and it is a sad lot in comparison with what the promises of democratic theorists would lead us to expect—but they have also destroyed the planet to an extent that dramatically outstrips all other political regimes,[26] and they are involved in an unprecedented attack on the living beings of the planet, the intensity of which is criminal. Making human beings the unconditional center of the political process leads to the systematic genocide of species, an astronomical proliferation of suffering, and suicide on the part of all those who have not been eradicated by other means. From a Buddhist point of view, for example, modern Western civilization leads not to (commercial) collapse but rather to absolute (ethical) breakdown. The dissolution of Communist regimes has led capitalist regimes to believe that they have definitively won the game, when in fact they have definitively lost, and their loss is made all the more resounding by the lack of visible opponents who would force them to revise their judgments and avoid final collapse. At the same time, we are convinced that a theocratic regime is necessarily and fundamentally rooted in the mother of all lies, namely that of the existence of God or gods—which is to say that "disembodied minds" will ultimately find a place in this somewhat vague ensemble.

2. The latter claim leads to the second objection. It is more difficult to respond to this objection because it is squarely opposed to one of the ontological pillars of our culture. Do "disembodied

minds" exist? Such a question calls not only for an anthropo-
logical or historical response but also for an empirical one that
demonstrates that such minds are more than mere phantasms,
autosuggestions, or psychological manipulations. In *all* societies,
including those of Europe and North America, there are isolated
individuals, male and female, who have relationships with such
"disembodied minds" and who organize their lives (and those of
numerous other people) around them. To consider these intermediaries to be charlatans or unscrupulous manipulators makes
sense only if one adopts a desperately *non*empirical attitude, a
dogmatic attitude that is set against the available evidence. We
should note that acknowledging the *existence* of such minds does
nothing to ascertain their *nature*; these are two distinct questions.
There are plenty of con men one might approach on this subject,
none of whom have a satisfactory response to this question: there
are some very bad doctors, but none of them will challenge the
overall usefulness of medicine, just as no pseudo-artist has ever
denied the existence of genuine artists. In fact, all peoples, virtu-
ally without exception, make room for "disembodied minds" and
have developed diverse modes of commerce with them; Westerners constitute the sole exception—and they have done so only
since the eighteenth century. Strictly speaking, there are only two
possible explanations for this problematic exception. The first is
that Westerners are the first to have detached the errors of existence from "disembodied minds," which has made Westerners
bellwethers of progress. The second is that Westerners are the
only ones blind enough to truly believe that such beings do not

exist and to have succeeded in the disastrous exploit of cutting off communication with them. Western intellectuals do not simply privilege the first response; they go so far as to deny that there can be any other response. Today this neocolonialist attitude is based less on a sense of racial superiority over other peoples than on the assumption of cultural and historical superiority. One finds a paradigmatic and caricatured instance of this attitude in contemporary cognitive anthropology. One of the constitutive principles of this discipline is that of cognitive universals. Human beings are superior primates who share the same cognitive system regardless of the culture in which they evolve. Comparing different cultures makes it possible to identify the cognitive characteristics that are proper to *Homo sapiens* above and beyond the cultural transformations that different cultures may have introduced. The best-known example of this approach is the study initiated by Brent Berlin and Paul Kay in the 1960s, which showed that all peoples throughout the world perceived colors in the same way, independently of the vocabulary they used to describe them. Experimental testing shows that a Dani of New Guinea, who has only two words for color (the equivalents of *black* and *white*), perceives the same colors as an English person, who has hundreds of color terms in his vocabulary.[27] Naturally the only exception to this methodology is precisely the perception of "disembodied minds"—and that remains completely arbitrary.

3. The hypothesis of "disembodied minds" is also difficult to maintain because it appears to be squarely opposed to the kind of rationalism that we place above all else. Thus, there is some

value in demonstrating that it is not the willingness but rather the refusal to accord any importance to "disembodied minds" that is irrational. Paul Feyerabend was delighted to show that rationalist denial is intrinsically fragile. He paints a portrait of the rationalist as a sumo wrestler who wants to win at any cost. He shows the rationalist to be a dominator who constantly uses nonrational arguments to make his point of view win out. This rationalist-sumo is a political strategist and is far from being a player who scrupulously follows the rules, although he tries to pass himself off as one. He is prepared to transgress the rules of rationality in order to make rationality victorious; here rationality is at once a goal to be attained, an asceticism to be practiced, and a pressure tactic to be employed against its adversaries. The rationalist-sumo plays several games at once, and his rationalism is as much a moral value as an intellectual position. This warrior-rationalist is also distinctive for a combination of ignorance and bad faith with regard to the traditions that he seeks to destroy, and he always presents nonrationalist traditions (or those traditions that he claims are nonrationalist) in a distorted way. In this connection, Paul Feyerabend, whom I have already mentioned, writes that astrology bores him to death but that the way in which Western scientists dismiss it reflects the dogmatic fashion in which they treat subjects that clearly lie outside their sphere of competence. This is particularly true in the case of the rejection of traditional medicine. The situation is aggravated by philosopher-mercenaries who legitimize rationalist-sumos. In the face of a bellicose dogmatic rationalism, Feyerabend envisions a critical rationalism to be carried out along the lines of assize courts with procedures that permit the parties to proclaim and defend their respective interests. He criticizes the rationalists in the very name of rationalism. Feyerabend should not be taken too much at face value; on several occasions, he has distanced himself from such a position and has asserted the right to be wrong and even to change his mind on the matter. The true rationalist is one who does not hesitate to be challenged by his own empirical experiences, not one who would rather not see (or, worse, who dogmatically dismisses) the empirical evidence that refutes his beliefs. This is the position that William James called "radical empiricism": "To be radical, an empiricism must neither admit into its constructions any element that is not directly experienced, nor exclude from them any element that is directly experienced."[28]

Are There Any Alternatives?

Those who reject factory farming on ethical grounds, environmental grounds, or grounds of public health are united in their aim to abandon the practice. We are far from doing so. The boycott undertaken by vegetarians has had little impact because there are too few opponents of factory farming to pose a threat to the meat industry. The forced closing of meat factories is a fanciful dream in the context of liberal democracies, which are hardly in a position to challenge the interests of the most powerful commercial organizations. Even a popular referendum, assuming that one could be arranged, would at best bring about mixed results:

most people are stuck in a rationality of the short term and prefer a poor-quality steak at a cheap price to ethical husbandry practices (and here I am not even addressing the fact that the meat has practically no nutritional value). The situation is precisely the same for the widespread destruction of our ecosystems and global warming. A democracy simply cannot enter into *long-term* decisions pertaining to the common good that so clearly run counter to particular *short-term* material interests. Here we clearly encounter the limits of Western democracies. Of course, the problem is not new. It has arisen over and over again ever since the beginnings of liberal democracy. It is precisely what the Marxists were talking about when they spoke of alienation. Rousseau expressed an early intuition about this when he stated that people must be forced to be free.[29] But how do you force someone to be free? Rousseau invents the notion of public opinion to respond to this question. But when public opinion makes a choice that clearly goes against the public's own interest, what can one do? Democracy itself runs up against the tyranny of the majority, a phenomenon that it fully repudiates and tries to get past with the notion (a pretty meaningless one at that) of individual liberty. This problem is not new; it has been discussed by many thinkers.[30] All constitutional democracies have put in place systems for regulating the "general will" (e.g., parliaments), but such systems remain largely ineffectual with regard to the exigencies that interest us here (effective environmental measures and the abolition of factory farming). One might envision a dictatorial procedure carried out by "wise" individuals who "temporarily" make "good" decisions in an authoritarian manner for the good of all, but history has always shown that the "wise" individual is never as wise as he or she should be. The Marxists, who have been more lucid on this point, invented the party and the "dictatorship of the proletariat"—with well-known catastrophic results. How are we to get out of this dilemma? My proposal for a nonreligious constitutional theocracy is based on the assumptions that the problems encountered by Western democracies are a product of the closed political space in which these democracies have evolved and that there is a need to open this space to "disembodied minds," just as it has been done in shamanic systems. This does not mean granting power to these minds or their appointed intermediaries but rather requiring ourselves to take into account what they say before making a decision. Thus, it is a matter of inventing forms of democracy that are open to beings other than humans. This openness would have three major advantages: decisions would be more adequately grounded; they would possess a legitimacy that would involve the citizen; and they would provide a potent counterforce to commercial enterprise. Problems such as the imperative to end factory farming are ultimately so great that they stand in need of unorthodox allies in order to be addressed with a reasonable hope of success.

RATHER THAN FOCUSING on the ethical problem of the consumption of meat, which is really secondary, vegetarians ought to concentrate their efforts on the deeper moral problem of meat factories. They should also realize that the measures that they have traditionally employed have as good as no chance of success. Thus, they should be prepared to employ unconventional political strategies they have never attempted. The problem is that vegetarians do not take into account the need for radical political measures and the importance of forging strategic alliances with ethical carnivores as a way of achieving their goals. The singular crisis of a world that tolerates meat factories calls for a political response of unconventional magnitude—for this is the only response that can possibly succeed in the face of an exceptional situation that demands not simply means but ends. It is fanciful to think that contemporary Western democracies can ban meat factories because these democracies function in a manner that absolutely precludes such a measure. Günther Anders understood very well that, as regards the atomic bomb and the automation of society, contemporary democracies live beyond their intellectual means and jeopardize the entire world with their ethical excesses, thereby rendering the prospect of any deep change utterly illusory. Raymond Ruyer, for his part, had the insight that only those societies that open up a political space for "disembodied minds" have a chance of surviving catastrophe—not simply by indicating the best *course* to follow (or, as he makes quite clear in his writings, the best *voices* to heed) but rather by constituting a power outside the human sphere that stands alone in possessing the legitimacy to truly change things. We modern democrats have forgotten that one of the basic functions of the king was to establish a political connection with the suprahuman to resolve conflicts between opposing factions. But for all that, it is not a matter of returning to some form of monarchy, which has long since lost all credibility and has been relegated to the theater of the grotesque and the gossip pages of glossy magazines.

Philosophers themselves struggle with this task. They often suffer from what one might call the "a posteriori realist illusion." One tends to believe that the most likely possibilities are the only ones that actually exist inasmuch as hindsight gives rise to the impression that the most likely possibilities are the only ones that ever actually come to pass, and yet this is an error in reasoning. One of the key features of a major event is that the event generates its own plausibility in the very moment that it takes place. It may well be a truism, but the best way to establish that a phenomenon is plausible is to make it come to pass. Today, at time t' it would be difficult for someone to predict what will happen at future time $t' + q$ unless that person were a professional psychic, in which case he or she would have left philosophy behind. Detached critical reflection would have to lead any thinker attempting to maintain a cool head to the conclusion that the unthinkable is always possible and that anything can happen. Nassim Nicholas Taleb has recently offered a convincing example of such a possibility with his theory of the black swan in the economic sphere; Taleb goes so far as to maintain that the most improbable is not only plausible but downright certain provided we take into account a sufficiently large time frame.[31] Thus, the claim that a nonreligious constitutional theocracy that ascribes an important role to shamans has no chance of coming into existence has exactly the same value as the claim that it does have a chance. Moreover, philosophy has no reason to take the form of an autobiographical exercise. My own opinions count for little. It is more interesting to test ideas that are a priori counterintuitive and push them to the limit in order to assess their plausibility. We are often surprised. All too often we reject important ideas because we let ourselves be influenced by prevailing beliefs or by the beliefs of people we admire the most. In spite of their best efforts, philosophers fail to exceed the fundamental limitations of human intelligence; and even if one day we will have to envision the possibility of "genetically modified philosophers" (GMP), we have not yet reached that point. Philosophers who write in order to provide themselves with reassurance ought to marry, consult a psychiatrist, or change their profession. And, as Feyerabend wisely states, "while you may *use* certain ideas you need not *accept* them."[32] You can promote ideas you do not support as a way of bolstering the ones you believe.

In this postface, I have tried to show that the problem of meat factories is essentially a political problem that cannot be solved within the ordinary framework of Western liberal democracies, and I have suggested that nonreligious, constitutional shamanic theocracies might provide a solution by mobilizing a space of legitimacy, "disembodied minds," that has been neutralized by modernity—yet, the rejection of religion having been so widely embraced, a space of this kind is simply too far removed from the prevailing beliefs of our time to be given serious attention. Today it is incumbent upon us to recognize that the means typically mobilized by Western liberal democracies are incapable of solving the extraordinary ethical problems that confront us. The limits of

our intelligence, our technological activism, and our political im-
maturity are leading us to an impasse that can be overcome only
through recourse to strategies that lie outside accepted norms—
that is, strategies that are a priori *extravagant*. What I have proposed can certainly be characterized in these terms, although in
itself that is not a serious objection. The idea of a constitutional
theocracy is not as absurd as it might appear at first blush; I propose a theocracy without clergy or religion, a federation organized
around local shamans who communicate with "disembodied
minds" (whatever these minds may actually turn out to be, though
even a little empirical investigation will confirm their existence),
not because deities can miraculously save us but because we do not
possess the intelligence to escape our catastrophic situation on our
own, and all available cognitive resources must be mobilized to
achieve this aim. I am prepared to discuss other options, but I am
unaware of any. I am aware that the idea of installing a nonreligious theocratic regime is unthinkable today, but that is no reason
to refrain from discussing it: the first theorists of democracy were
not taken seriously in their own time, and we have seen what
ensued from their ideas. Just as paradoxically, climate change may
turn out to help those who seek to close the meat factories. When
people finally understand the significance of a two-degree increase
in temperature, they will be ready to get involved in activities that
strike us today as far-fetched. Climate change signals the end of
liberal Western democracies as we have known them, but precious
few among us have become aware of this.

Notes

Translator's Preface

1. Martin Heidegger, "The Question Concerning Technology," in *The Question Concerning Technology and Other Essays*, ed. William Lovitt (New York: Random House, 1977), 35 (translation altered).

2. For the sake of simplicity, I follow Lestel in referring simply to "vegetarians" as a shorthand for "vegetarians and/or vegans." Also, as Lestel notes in his discussion, the focus here is not those who are vegetarians for reasons of health or environmental concern but exclusively those who embrace vegetarianism on moral grounds.

3. Lestel argues for such an ethics of responsibility toward animals not only in this text but also in *L'animal est l'avenir de l'homme* (The animal is the future of the human) (Paris: Fayard, 2010). I have developed my own views on this question in *Animals and the Moral Community: Mental Life, Moral Status, and Kinship* (New York: Columbia University Press, 2008) and *Animals and the Limits of Postmodernism* (New York: Columbia University Press, 2013). I critically examine Lestel's arguments for ethical carnivorism in the latter text (218–27).

4. Lestel, *L'animal est l'avenir de l'homme*, 125.

5. Lestel is nothing if not a person keenly in tune with the spirit of irony. Several years ago he and I were walking along the promenade overlooking

Sydney Harbour, and I asked him why he advocates eating animals but not our fellow humans as a way of discharging our infinite debt to the living. He smiled a Cheshire Cat grin and said that he would be most delighted to eat *me*.

6. I am indebted to Matt Chrulew, Jeffrey Bussolini, Hollis Taylor, an anonymous reader for Columbia University Press, and of course Dominique Lestel for various forms of assistance and inspiration in connection with this translation. My sincere thanks also go to Anne McCoy for her superb supervision of this project and Annie Barva for her outstanding editing work.

A Sort of Apéritif

1. Estiva Reus and Antoine Comiti, "Abolir la viande," *Cahiers antispécistes* 29 (February 2008), http://www.cahiers-antispecistes.org/.

2. The literature on this subject is immense but often quite repetitive. In order to understand ethical vegetarianism from the inside, I recommend a passionate book: Kerry Walters and Lisa Portmess, eds., *Ethical Vegetarianism: From Pythagoras to Peter Singer* (New York: State University of New York Press, 1999).

3. It goes without saying that I have never received so much as a penny from the meat industry. I already have many enemies; it is pointless to saddle myself with additional friends of a compromising nature.

Appetizer: How Does One Recognize an Ethical Vegetarian?

1. George Bernard Shaw, who was a vegetarian out of necessity, regretted not being one for ethical reasons.

2. Paul Amato and Sonia Partridge, *The New Vegetarians: Promoting Health and Protecting Life* (Heidelberg: Springer, 1989), 98.

3. Carol J. Adams, *The Sexual Politics of Meat: A Feminist–Vegetarian Critical Theory*, rev. ed. (New York: Continuum/Bloomsbury Academic, 2010).

Notes

Hors d'Oeuvre: A Short History of Vegetarian Practices

1. Colin Spencer, *The Heretic's Feast: A History of Vegetarianism* (London: Fourth Estate, 1993).

2. Marcel Détienne, *Les jardins d'Adonis: La mythologie des aromates en Grèce* (Paris: Gallimard, 1972).

First Course: Some (Good) Reasons *Not* to Become an Ethical Vegetarian

1. John Lawrence Hill, *The Case for Vegetarianism: Philosophy for a Small Planet* (Lanham, Md.: Rowman and Littlefield, 1996).

2. Jeremy Narby, *Intelligence in Nature: An Inquiry Into Knowledge* (New York: Tarcher/Penguin, 2005).

3. Anthony Trewavas, "How Plants Learn," *Proceedings of the National Academy of Sciences USA* 96 (1999): 4218.

4. Narby, *Intelligence in Nature*, 94.

5. Quoted in Florence Burgat, "'Humanisation' biologique des animaux (remarques sur les xénogreffes)," chapter 3 of *Liberté et inquietude de la vie animale* (Paris: Kime, 2006), 47–58.

6. As phrased by Oron Catts in Stephanie Kramer, "Interview with Oron Catts: Victimless Leather," *Urban Times*, April 13, 2012, https://urbantimes .co/2012/04/interview-oron-catts-victimless-leather/comment-page-1/.

7. See, for example, J. Baird Callicott, "Animal Liberation: A Triangular Affair," in *The Animal Rights/Environmental Ethics Debate: The Environmental Perspective*, ed. Eugene C. Hargrove (Albany: State University of New York Press, 1992), 55–57.

8. Clément Rosset, *Le principe de cruauté* (Paris: Minuit, 1988), 17–20.

9. Here I am playing, in a manner that is certainly somewhat ironic, on the distinction made by the Norwegian philosopher Arne Naess between "superficial ecology" and "deep ecology."

10. I thank Vinciane Despret for this reference because I have not been intelligent enough to read Donna Haraway for myself.

11. Gary Snyder, *A Place in Space: Ethics, Aesthetics, and Watersheds: New and Selected Prose* (Washington, D.C.: Counterpoint, 1995), 70.

Second Course: The Ethics of the Carnivore

1. My interest in this notion of commemoration was inspired by Vinciane Despret over two bottles of wine, and I thank her for it. One can never overestimate the importance of the grape in the history of Western thought, and I think it is worth bearing this in mind in the current discussion of vegetarianism.

2. Cora Diamond, "Eating Meat and Eating People," in *Animal Rights: Current Debates and New Directions*, ed. Cass R. Sunstein and Martha C. Nussbaum (Oxford: Oxford University Press, 2004), 93–107.

3. As far as I know, in every case of criminal cannibalism to have made the news in the second half of the twentieth century, the cannibals have always been male, never female. I offer this important detail to feminists, who may see in it yet *another* symptom of the monstrosity of men.

4. In the West, the Stoics went very far in this direction. The love of fate that they proclaimed is the clearest expression of this: love that to which you are obligated. But one might go even further and say: find very positive aspects in that to which you are obligated, such that even if you have the choice, you would still choose that which is imposed upon you at this moment.

5. Paul Shepard, *The Tender Carnivore and the Sacred Game* (1973; reprint, Athens: University of Georgia Press, 1998).

6. Avital Ronell, *Crack Wars: Literature, Addiction, Mania* (Lincoln: University of Nebraska Press, 2004).

7. Ernst Bloch, *Traces*, trans. Anthony A. Nassar (Stanford, Calif.: Stanford University Press, 2006).

Notes

8. Some would have said "deepen" rather than "extend" our awareness. Metaphors of depth always seem to me eminently suspect, and I prefer topographic and geographic metaphors. Someday I will have to return to this point.

9. Vegetarians, especially ethical ones, will naturally dispute this distinction. They may say, for example, that I am deploying a Machiavellian strategy designed to divide and conquer.

10. Claude Lévi-Strauss, "La leçon de sagesse des vaches folles," *La Repubblica*, November 24, 1996.

A Sort of Dessert

1. Ernst Bloch, *The Principle of Hope*, 3 vols., trans. Neville Plaice, Stephen Plaice, and Paul Knight (Cambridge, Mass.: MIT Press, 1995).

2. Hans Jonas, *The Imperative of Responsibility: In Search of an Ethics for the Technological Age* (Chicago: University of Chicago Press, 1985).

Postface

1. To my knowledge, theorists of the posthuman and the transhuman are the first and only ones to have taken this problem seriously and to have proposed the biological and technological growth of human intelligence in order to solve it.

2. Günther Anders's work can be found in numerous essays.

3. Günther Anders, *L'obsolescence de l'homme: Sur l'âme à l'époque de la deuxième révolution industrielle*, trans. Christoph David (Paris: Éditions de l'Encyclopédie des nuisances, 2002), 31–32.

4. Much later and independently of Anders, Slavoj Žižek will propose a related analysis according to which Western liberal democracies do not ultimately accept the fact that the choices, the "good" choices, have already been made. A clear example of this situation is the institutional coup d'état

that took place in France in 2001 on the occasion of the referendum on Europe [i.e., the decision whether to remain in the European Union]. The majority of French people voted no, but the government at the time explained this defeat by taking the position that its pedagogy had not been adequate to explain the "good" choice and . . . by opting for adhesion to Europe! The problem of Western liberal democracies is precisely that they are *not* democracies.

5. Anders, 32.

6. Ibid., 121.

7. Ibid., 276–77.

8. Futurists always take a very different approach to the future; rather than determining which is the most likely future, they distill the opinions of experts regarding what the future might be. The outcome of what was once thought of as the Delphi method (particularly by Herman Kahn, one of the great U.S. theorists of the equilibrium of terror) has always been shown to be false. I think it is more interesting to seek radical alternatives that have the least chance of coming to pass, even the most counterintuitive ones, and to consider the responses that might be offered to such situations if they were to arise.

9. See, for example, John Seed, Joanna Macy, Pat Fleming, and Arne Naess, *Thinking Like a Mountain: Towards a Council of All Beings* (Philadelphia: New Society, 1988), and Joanna Macy, "Council of All Beings," in *Encyclopedia of Nature and Religion*, ed. Bron Taylor (New York: Continuum, 2005), 425–29.

10. For example, in *Cholera et temps: Essai politico-psychologique* (Paris: Maren Sell, 2007), Peter Sloterdijk makes this approach the "second macropolitical mission of the future" (64).

11. According to the theory of the multiverse, we live in a world in which there is a plurality of universes. The Russian cosmologist Andreï Linde argued for the plausibility of such a theory at a conference at MIT on March 18, 2014.

12. Consider what nowadays is called the ontological turn in anthropology. For a critical and interesting discussion of this turn, see Morton Axel

Pedersen, "Common Nonsense: A Review of Certain Recent Reviews of the 'Ontological Turn,'" *Anthropology of the Century*, no. 5 (October 2012), http://aotcpress.com/articles/common_nonsense/.

13. Recent work on shamanism is particularly interesting. See, for example, Graham Harvey, *Animism: Respecting the Living World* (London: Hurst, 2005); Nurit Bird-David, "'Animism' Revisited: Personhood, Environment, and Relational Epistemology," *Current Anthropology* 40 (February 1999): S67–S91; and, more recently, Eduardo Kohn, *How Forests Think: Toward an Anthropology Beyond the Human* (Berkeley: University of California Press, 2013).

14. Raymond Ruyer, *Les cent prochains siècles: Le destin historique de l'homme selon la Nouvelle Gnose américaine* (Paris: Fayard, 1977).

15. Ruyer develops this idea at length in chapter 12 of his book *Les cent prochains siècles*, "Profil des peuples long vivants au-delà des cent prochains siècles" (Profile of long-living peoples beyond the next hundred centuries), 268–315, which is the source of all passages cited in this paragraph.

16. Raymond Ruyer, *Les nourritures psychiques: La politique du bonheur* (Paris: Calmann-Lévy, 1975).

17. Paul Feyerabend, *Against Method: Outline of an Anarchistic Theory of Knowledge*, in *Analyses of Theories and Methods of Physics and Psychology*, ed. Michael Radner and Stephen Winokur (Minneapolis: University of Minnesota Press, 1970), 17–130 (reprint, New York: New Left Books, 1975).

18. Here I call a "shaman" every healer who appeals to "disembodied minds" for guidance.

19. *Translator's note*: Here Lestel uses the term *commercer avec* and reminds the reader that "in French the term *commercer* has a broader meaning than simply engaging in commerce in the modern sense of the term; it means 'to have an ongoing relationship with.'"

20. Here I will not go into detail on questions such as the number of shamans, how they are to be described (other than to say that they have a relationship to disembodied minds), how they are to be chosen, who chooses them, and so on. There are many categories of shaman, including benevolent and malevolent ones. I am not saying that such a system will be

perfect (there is no hope of that) but that it will be better for addressing the environmental and ethical problems that concern us here, problems that are quickly going to become much more central than those of social division sensu stricto. (At the same time, we must not forget problems of social division inasmuch as they are an essential part of the problem.)

21. The Iroquois League, known as the Five Nations, originally consisted of the Mohawk, the Oneida, the Onondaga, the Cayuga, and the Seneca. In 1722, the Tuscarora joined, and the Iroquois League became the Six Nations. This democratic political association was organized around an oral constitution, the Great Binding Law or Gayanashagowa. Enacted in the twelfth century, it was revised in 1720 and is composed of 117 paragraphs.

22. Vine Deloria (1933–2005) is one Amerindian intellectual who has taken a position on this matter. Deloria maintains explicitly that only indigenous visions and practices can save the planet from impending disaster.

23. It is precisely the religious aspect of Buddhism, its organization around a clergy, that I consider to be a problem, even though this aspect also brings with it respect for living beings.

24. Note that what I am proposing here has nothing to do with New Age ideas, which are grounded in a primitive animism, a puerile occultism, and a liberal ideology of human potential.

25. For an account of the regime of the mullahs that avoids caricature, see, for example, Olivier Roy, "Une théocratie constitutionnelle: Les institutions de la République islamique d'Iran," *Politique Etrangère* 52, no. 2 (1987): 327–38.

26. Communist regimes may well have done even worse; in this connection, the catastrophic situation in China speaks volumes.

27. Brent Berlin and Paul Kay, *Basic Color Terms: Their Universality and Evolution* (Berkeley: University of California Press, 1969).

28. William James, "A World of Pure Experience" (1912), in *The Works of William James: Essays in Radical Empiricism*, ed. Fredson Bowers and Ignis Skrupskelis (Cambridge, Mass.: Harvard University Press, 1976), 22.

29. Jean-Jacques Rousseau, *The Social Contract* (1762), book 1, chap. 7.

30. One might cite, for example, Benjamin Constant, *Principles of Politics Applicable to All Governments* (1815); Alexis de Tocqueville, *Democracy in America* (1835), book 1; and John Stuart Mill, *On Liberty* (1859).

31. Nassim Nicholas Taleb, *The Black Swan: The Impact of the Highly Improbable*, 2nd ed. (New York: Random House, 2010).

32. Paul Feyerabend, *Three Dialogues on Knowledge* (Oxford: Blackwell, 1991), 50.

Bibliography

Adams, Carol J. *The Sexual Politics of Meat: A Feminist–Vegetarian Critical Theory*. Rev. ed. New York: Continuum/Bloomsbury Academic, 2010.

Amato, Paul, and Sonia Partridge. *The New Vegetarians: Promoting Health and Protecting Life*. Heidelberg: Springer, 1989.

Anders, Günther. *L'obsolescence de l'homme: Sur l'âme à l'époque de la deuxième révolution industrielle*. Translated by Christoph David. Paris: Éditions de l'Encyclopédie des nuisances, 2002.

Berlin, Brent, and Paul Kay. *Basic Color Terms: Their Universality and Evolution*. Berkeley: University of California Press, 1969.

Bird-David, Nurit. "'Animism' Revisited: Personhood, Environment, and Relational Epistemology." *Current Anthropology* 40 (February 1999): S67–S91.

Bloch, Ernst. *The Principle of Hope*. 3 vols. Translated by Neville Plaice, Stephen Plaice, and Paul Knight. Cambridge, Mass.: MIT Press, 1995.

——. *Traces*. Translated by Anthony A. Nassar. Stanford, Calif.: Stanford University Press, 2006.

Burgat, Florence. *Liberté et inquiétude de la vie animale*. Paris: Kimé, 2006.

Callicott, J. Baird. "Animal Liberation: A Triangular Affair." In *The Animal Rights/Environmental Ethics Debate: The Environmental Perspective*, edited by Eugene C. Hargrove, 37–69. Albany: State University of New York Press, 1992.

Bibliography

Détienne, Marcel. *Les jardins d'Adonis: La mythologie des aromates en Grèce.* Paris: Gallimard, 1972.

Diamond, Cora. "Eating Meat and Eating People." In *Animal Rights: Current Debates and New Directions,* edited by Cass R. Sunstein and Martha C. Nussbaum, 93–107. Oxford: Oxford University Press, 2004.

Feyerabend, Paul. *Against Method: Outline of an Anarchistic Theory of Knowledge.* In *Analyses of Theories and Methods of Physics and Psychology,* edited by Michael Radner and Stephen Winokur, 17–130. Minneapolis: University of Minnesota Press, 1970. Reprint. New York: New Left Books, 1975.

——. *Three Dialogues on Knowledge.* Oxford: Blackwell, 1991.

Harvey, Graham. *Animism: Respecting the Living World.* London: Hurst, 2005.

Heidegger, Martin. "The Question Concerning Technology." In *The Question Concerning Technology and Other Essays,* edited by William Lovitt, 3–35. New York: Random House, 1977.

Hill, John Lawrence. *The Case for Vegetarianism: Philosophy for a Small Planet.* Lanham, Md.: Rowman and Littlefield, 1996.

James, William. "A World of Pure Experience" (1912). In *The Works of William James: Essays in Radical Empiricism,* edited by Fredson Bowers and Ignis Skrupskelis, 21–44. Cambridge, Mass.: Harvard University Press, 1976.

Jonas, Hans. *The Imperative of Responsibility: In Search of an Ethics for the Technological Age.* Chicago: University of Chicago Press, 1985.

Kohn, Eduardo. *How Forests Think: Toward an Anthropology Beyond the Human.* Berkeley: University of California Press, 2013.

Kramer, Stephanie. "Interview with Oron Catts: Victimless Leather." *Urban Times,* April 13, 2012. https://urbantimes.co/2012/04/interview-oron-catts-victimless-leather/comment-page-1/.

Lestel, Dominique. *L'animal est l'avenir de l'homme.* Paris: Fayard, 2010.

Lévi-Strauss, Claude. "La leçon de sagesse des vaches folles." *La Repubblica,* November 24, 1996.

Bibliography

Macy, Joanna. "Council of All Beings." In *Encyclopedia of Nature and Religion*, edited by Bron Taylor, 425–29. New York: Continuum, 2005.

Narby, Jeremy. *Intelligence in Nature: An Inquiry Into Knowledge*. New York: Tarcher/Penguin, 2005.

Pedersen, Morton Axel. "Common Nonsense: A Review of Certain Recent Reviews of the 'Ontological Turn.'" *Anthropology of the Century*, no. 5 (October 2012). http://aotcpress.com/articles/common_nonsense/.

Reus, Estiva, and Antoine Comiti. "Abolir la viande." *Cahiers antispécistes* 29 (February 2008). http://cahiers-antispecistes.org/.

Ronell, Avital. *Crack Wars: Literature, Addiction, Mania*. Lincoln: University of Nebraska Press, 2004.

Rosset, Clément. *Le principe de cruauté*. Paris: Minuit, 1988.

Roy, Olivier. "Une théocratie constitutionnelle: Les institutions de la République islamique d'Iran." *Politique etrangère* 52, no. 2 (1987): 327–38.

Ruyer, Raymond. *Les cent prochains siècles: Le destin historique de l'homme selon la Nouvelle Gnose américaine*. Paris: Fayard, 1977.

——. *Les nourritures psychiques: La politique du bonheur*. Paris: Calmann-Lévy, 1975.

Seed, John, Joanna Macy, Pat Fleming, and Arne Naess, *Thinking Like a Mountain: Towards a Council of All Beings*. Philadelphia: New Society, 1988.

Shepard, Paul. *The Tender Carnivore and the Sacred Game*. 1973. Reprint. Athens: University of Georgia Press, 1998.

Sloterdijk, Peter. *Cholera et temps: Essai politico-psychologique*. Paris: Maren Sell, 2007.

Snyder, Gary. *A Place in Space: Ethics, Aesthetics, and Watersheds: New and Selected Prose*. Washington, D.C.: Counterpoint, 1995.

Spencer, Colin. *The Heretic's Feast: A History of Vegetarianism*. London: Fourth Estate, 1993.

Steiner, Gary. *Animals and the Limits of Postmodernism*. New York: Columbia University Press, 2013.

Bibliography

———. *Animals and the Moral Community: Mental Life, Moral Status, and Kinship*. New York: Columbia University Press, 2008.

Taleb, Nassim Nicholas. *The Black Swan: The Impact of the Highly Improbable*. 2nd ed. New York: Random House, 2010.

Trewavas, Anthony. "How Plants Learn." *Proceedings of the National Academy of Sciences USA* 96 (1999): 4216–18.

Walters, Kerry, and Lisa Portmess, eds. *Ethical Vegetarianism: From Pythagoras to Peter Singer*. New York: State University of New York Press, 1999.